TELL ME ABOUT IT

For information address:
Hyperion, 77 West 66th Street,
New York, New York 10023-6298.

Library of Congress Cataloging-in-Publication Data
Hax, Carolyn.
Tell me about it : lying, sulking, and getting fat
and 56 other things not to do while looking
for love / by Carolyn Hax.—1st ed.
p. cm.
ISBN: 0-7868-6673-X
1. Dating (Social customs)   2. Man-woman
relationships.   I. Title
HQ801.H3715 2001
646.7'7—dc21   00-040703

Illustration on page 4 by Nick Galifianakis,
© Nick Galifianakis

FIRST EDITION
10 9 8 7 6 5 4 3

TELL ME ABOUT IT

Lying, Sulking, Getting Fat
and 56 Other Things Not to Do
While Looking for Love

Carolyn Hax

talk miramax books

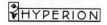

INTRODUCTION

—

Before I talk about you, a bit about me: I am not a doctor or psychologist or trained observer/opiner of any sort. I write a newspaper advice column regardless—it's called "Tell Me About It" and appears in the *Washington Post* and in syndication—and I am well aware this is a semiweekly act of gall on my part. I often rationalize my job by explaining that I have still-married parents and three sisters whom I not only love and respect but also like; a husband of six years whom I'd marry again (I'd wear a different dress though); old friends, and new, who are at once relaxing, entertaining and enlightening company; an earnest but not always successful desire to learn from my many and varied mistakes; and a dog that forgives me for everything and in doing so reminds me of the simple beauty in that. It's the I'm-stable-therefore-I-am argument, life as education. Not good enough? I was trained to write—how's that.

And, of course, read. I spend most of my time reading now, as people send to me, night and day, on paper or through the ether, these stunning leaps of faith in a total stranger whom they trust to answer their deepest most private most personal questions despite (or is it thanks to?) her aforesaid "issues" with gall. Bless them. I answer some of them, a small percentage really; I try to help and at least not hurt . . . much, and to find some humor, somewhere, in all this deathly seriousness we instill in our daily personal lives. In return I've gotten loyal readers and thoughtful debates and some hate mail that could blow-dry your hair. These are things I expected to come with the job.

What I didn't expect, what came as a surprise (though it wouldn't have, if I'd actually given this job some thought beyond, "Cool, I could do that," before I suggested it), was the daily education. What better way to learn about people than to let them speak for themselves? Multiple times a day, I get a detailed accounting of what people do and why, and what happens as a result of their actions. Specifically, what bad thing happens as a result—I write an advice column, not some rah-rah alumni class notes. Looking at all of these bad results over all the days, weeks, now years I've done this column, I noticed something: The letters I've received are a virtual catalogue of the most counterproductive ways to interact with other human beings. (Beginning with writing to advice columnists. Yuk yuk.) Not just the wrong ways romantically, either: platonically, too, and professionally, parentally and every-other-ly. That in itself taught me something, that romantic miseries can't be grouped, catalogued and neatly filed away under "The Only Part of My Life that Sucks." They seem to work more as the canary in our psychic coalmine. When we have substantial problems, our attractiveness, and specifically our mate-worthiness, is often the first bird to go.

Not that we really notice. Enter the second major theme that runs through my mail, the often breathtaking absence of self-awareness. We may be fully aware that we're not living in a romance novel, but we're also slow to make any connections that might incriminate ourselves. We'd rather not know that men don't ask for our phone numbers because we turn every conversation into an opportunity to rant bitterly about society's warped view of weight . . . because we're defensive about the extra pounds we're carrying . . . because we keep eating even when we're not hungry . . . because food provides a certain measure of comfort (though risibly false) during this self-loathing stage we seem to be in. Making that connection means telling ourselves something we don't want to hear—"I'm lonely, angry and fat"—so we write to an advice columnist instead: "I'm in my early twenties and I've had only two dates in my entire life. Where can I meet nice men?"

Coffee and denial are what get me out of bed some mornings, so I can appreciate the reluctance to follow such a soul-jarring train of thought. But the alternative—an unexamined, therefore unchanged, therefore perpetually unrewarding life—makes dealing with an uncomfortable truth start to sound appealing. Then the issue becomes *finding* that truth, another area at which we don't always excel.

It would be a lot easier if our friends would simply point out that if we didn't keep putting away six Twinkies at a clip, we wouldn't be quite so off-putting to the opposite sex, but saying that to a friend's face might be the only thing harder than admitting it to ourselves. So that's where people like me come in.

Something else I learned on the job: If you want some people to hate you at the molecular level, make these judgments in print. But before you join the God-you're-smug/arrogant/insufferable chorus, let me say that I'm not entirely unsympathetic to those who find me appalling (one cherished slam: "Do you have any professional training that gives you license to tell people to grow up and go to hell?"). I mean, who *am* I to judge? I've maintained since the beginning that I have no more expertise than your next-door neighbor. What I can offer, though, is the kind of honesty your next-door neighbor, who has to face you morning after morning after morning when she steps out to fetch her newspaper, can hardly afford.

I can also offer my intimate familiarity with uncomfortable personal truths. To be honest, it was unfair of me to suggest that readers' letters alone formed my catalogue of stupid relationship behavior. My own miscues during high school, college and my twenties were so vital to my "research" that, by my calculations, I am able to speak from experience on a full 36 percent of the things I'm about to advise you not to do. So here's the more accurate pitch: From moronic things I did, from what I had done to me, from what my readers have reported, from what my friends and family have been through and from sitting in a bar and watching you make an ass of yourself, here is everything people do (or everything I could think of by deadline) to scare Prince and/or Princess Charming away—plus excerpts from real letters about real mistakes in progress.

Note: I have tried to use he and/or she interchangeably to avoid sexist generalizations and any further use of "he and/or she." Therefore, any remaining sexist generalizations are purely coincidental, except where I've made them on purpose.

"Do you know of any classes or seminars on how to improve your dating skills?"

1

READING RELATIONSHIP BOOKS OR OTHERWISE TRAINING TO DATE

—

Humor me. Besides, this is a life book; I called it a dating book just to humor the marketing people.

If you're reading a book or taking a class that tells you what to do, *you* aren't telling you what to do. While that may seem like the point, wouldn't it be better if instead you found a way to trust your own voice? I'm not saying a book can't help you do that—but if you want a relationship education, read Jane Austen. Or Fitzgerald, Ellison, Waugh, Flannery O'Connor, the

Bible, a wicked *New Yorker* cartoon. Read *Anna Karenina* (but stay away from married Russian women and/or train platforms). What about movies? Plays? Music? Television? Would you rather 1) read a self-help book and think about you you you, or 2) read something with broader insights and capital-T think? Hint: Your next date hopes you choose option 2.

Virtually every cultural artifact we generate, high or low, electronic or newsprint or oil on canvas or oxidized bronze, makes some statement about human interaction. Spend your time absorbing these statements, making yourself smarter, placing yourself in their greater context. I'm not suggesting you can get romantic advice from a wall hanging. But you can get, say, a broader perspective on beauty—one that isn't limited to eight-foot tall, impossibly pneumatic supermodels who want nothing to do with you. You can widen your perspective, too, on other cultures, on the human experience, on the insignificance—and the profound and lasting power—of one individual life. You may still be screwed up, but at least you'll be interesting.

And if you are screwed up, thank you, you've kept us advice-dispensers in business. Since I stand to lose money on your 1) getting better, and 2) renouncing self-help, maybe you'll believe me when I say there are far more personal, constructive sources of help than self-help books. Start by talking with your (brighter, happier and more honest) friends—not just about your problems, but also about sports and life and the merits of Portuguese cheese. Listen for what makes people happy. Look up to someone and take note of what traits you admire. Scrutinize your family. See what you like, see what you don't like and see which ungainly mannerisms you've been saddled with by genes and osmosis and time. Look, hard, at the breakdowns of relationships past. See the pattern? No? See a therapist then, if your problems are tired, painful reruns and you don't understand why.

People think it's an admission of failure to seek outside help. I'd argue that it takes real strength to be able to say, "Hey, I'm missing something here, would you please have a look?" I'm not talking about five years of serotonin-reuptake inhibitors and a front-row seat in your navel (not unless the men in the white jumpsuits say you need them). I mean a few dedicated hours with someone—teacher, clergy, family doctor, company shrink—anyone whose judgment you respect. Find the recurring nightmare, face it, file it. Just don't foist it on us.

"She is very pretty, but she is fifty pounds overweight. Obviously, she needs to take better care of herself."

2

GETTING FAT

—

Yes, I know about stereotypes and body-image hangups and eating disorders and needing therapy to buy a swimsuit and I'm putting my fingers in my ears NAH NAH NAH NAH NAH NAH NAH, okay? Can I finish?

I said *get* fat not *be* fat and there is a difference, you know. (Though being fat is a liability, too, but more in how it relates to the former. I'll get to that.) The person who gets fat, who gets big as an adult from eating too much—as opposed to being lifelong big from the gift of big genes—does himself the grave disservice of making his "issues" immediately visible. And, therefore, highly run-away-fromable. Anyone who's ever gotten through a bad spell with an assist from Entenmann's and Pepperidge Farm knows that rapid pound acquisition is a classic sign of Shit Going On. (Or "In," I suppose.) Eating for comfort, eating as a reward, eating out of boredom, eating because you've given up: pounds, pounds, pounds, tons. And so while your mommy is programmed to recognize rapid weight gain as a sign of instability and ask you if you're okay (assuming she isn't a cupcake pusher herself), your average stranger is programmed to recognize this sign of instability and say, "No thanks." Get help if you need it, trace the cause of your caloric self-mutilation and stop it.

Which brings me to the other kind of big, the slow-metabolism, in-the-genes kind of big. I'm sorry. It's not anybody's fault. It gets rudely, judgmentally caught up in the same net people use to skim off the overeating and underdisciplined. It also gets used as a wholesale excuse by overeaters in denial, which doesn't help your cause. If it's any consolation, anyone who's paying attention can tell the difference, and see that someone who's fit and well-groomed and poised and oh by the way a size 14 is not in the depression-by-the-pound business. Unfortunately, few people in bars and clubs have ever been credibly accused of paying attention to subtleties (or obviousities, for that matter). But if you're going to pickup joints to be understood, I'd venture you have multiple problems of which bigness isn't the biggest.

"The only place it seems you can meet people is at clubs and bars, but there's no purpose in that if you don't drink or smoke and don't want to be with people who drink or smoke."

3

TURNING YOUR NOSE UP AT PICKUP JOINTS

—

If you think no one worth meeting would show up at a bar, how many other snooty generalizations are you making about people? Just curious.

I could fill an e-truck with complaints that this city or that city is a terrible place to meet people, when we all know there are millions of people in these same cities who don't have enough days in the week to spend with all the people they meet. Unless you spend the bulk of your time alone in your car with your windows rolled up, I think you need to let go of the delusion that your troubles all lie with location. Have you considered that it's not where you go but why you go, and what you do/say/radiate when you get there?

Bars are great places to get better at meeting people, for three reasons: crowds, darkness, alcohol. As long as you don't overindulge in any of them (getting sloppy here can get fatal), you've got the ideal conditions to practice practice practice your social moves. Afraid to walk right up to people? Start walking right up to people—or send them a drink and invite them to walk up to you. Mute with terror once you get there? Honesty can be so disarming: "I wanted to introduce myself but I tend to be shy, so I was hoping I could stand here and you'd have mercy and take over," or however you would say it. Stumped by the nuances of human nature? Grab a seat, observe the dramas and learn.

The object is to remove the "uh, will she think I'm hot?" sweating-and-stammering panic from initiating a social exchange. Why do you think people who are already seeing someone get hit on more than ever? Because they're not trying to get people to notice them, so they can talk to all kinds of people and stay perfectly relaxed. The best way for a single person to simulate that feeling is through quantity. In which situation will you be cooler: when you've spent all night noticing this one woman, wishing hoping wondering if you can work up enough courage to approach her, and then finally deciding to try; or approaching ten different women a night on the theory that you can't find the good ones if you never bother to look?

The beauty here is that if you fail at any of these introductions, you're no different from 90 percent of the people in the bar this very night who are themselves failing wholesale. Rejection? So? If you fail big, loud and ugly, you can always just leave. It's like penny-ante poker—a bar lets you venture only little bits of yourself, and that way you can make mistakes (and learn from them) without getting cleaned out. You don't expect to get rich, just maybe smarter and a little more confident each time — confident enough, eventually, to be the guy who can find new friends in a checkout line in Whoville.

"She'd tell me what this guy or that guy planned to do with her, such as flying her places, sharing expensive dinners, getting married, etc., all of which generally occurred between dates one through three. After that, they'd usually flee."

4

BEING DESPERATE, SEEMING DESPERATE OR EVEN STANDING NEXT TO DESPERATE WITHOUT A PROTECTIVE SUIT

—

Going to a bar solely to find a relationship? That's desperate. So is complaining to anyone, anywhere, about not having a *booooy*friend. So is clogging someone's answering machine, unless you have a crisp sense of humor about it. (See how it's done: Rent *Say Anything.* . . . See how it's not done: Rent *Swingers.*) More than five minutes' worth of makeup (excluding nail care)? Desperate. So is overthought or overtight or overover clothing. So are weepy 2 A.M. phone calls. So is believing your life is incomplete without a codependent, I mean, significant other. So is waiting for that significant other before you buy a home/travel/get nice stuff for your kitchen/start your life. So is consulting a dating manual (see number 1 on page 11). So is confiding in someone as if you've known her fifteen years when you've known her fifteen minutes. Calling a guy "honey" when you've gone on only four dates with him and you're not even remotely like those cool women in delis who call everybody "hon"? So desperate that I encourage anyone who encounters you to run away from you.

It may be hard to pin down "desperate" in one sentence, but that doesn't mean everyone in the room can't pin it down in one second. That's because we are all just animals, and animals are wired to sense—

accurately, swiftly, savagely—any weakness in a potential mate and to use that weakness as a way to thin the potential-mate herd. The scent that desperation gives off: "No one else has wanted me in a very long time."

"She had told me she was five foot five and
weighed about 140, but when I met her
I knew that although the height
was correct, her weight was off
by about fifty pounds."

5

SHOPPING ONLINE

—

This to me is like typing . . .

The sky is blue the sky is blue the sky is blue the sky is
blue . . . but every time I pick on Internet romance I
get at least five huffy letters that say I've failed to
appreciate that we're in a new age now, babe, and this
is the way it is.

Yes, it is. And the sky is STILL BLUE.

You can't see this person, so you don't know what she looks like. You can't hear this person, so you don't know if she sounds like Marvin the Martian. You can't smell this person, so you don't know if she bathes. Touch, taste . . . I'll leave those to you.

All these things you don't know and yet you're investing hours and hours in exploring each other's psyches (or, more accurately, what each of you *chooses to represent* of said psyche, which is a different ill altogether). So you form this person in your mind, and maybe you even fall for her in an e-kind of way, and then what? You meet her. You stand there. You marvel at how your body feels nothing for this person your mind has picked out for it. Hello, what do minds know about chemistry? Awkward moment! Awkward moment!

Humans come with five senses factory-installed to help them interact with their world. How bright is it to try to mate without using any of them? Phones and photos guarantee nothing about a person, so they don't count. And believe me, anyone who offends any of your senses is no one you want to live with.

Unfortunately, to someone with underdeveloped people skills, the senseless-mating idea, with all its faults, still sounds a lot more appealing than facing rejection in person. To someone with underdeveloped people skills, an eating-worms idea would sound more appealing than facing rejection in person. But while computers hold out the promise of a less judgmental way to meet people, the reality is (with romance, at least) that you're still going to be judged on the same face-to-face standards you always were—only later on in the process, when expectations are high. Painful.

Better to dispense with the swimsuit and congeniality contests upfront, even if that means a crash course in human interaction. There is some cruelty in this; the fewer people skills you have, the harder they are to develop, especially when you have social disorders that you can't just walk into a bar and fix. But again, she said, rubbing her face: Hoping to type your way to a wife (or worse, to import one from abroad, which astoundingly still occurs) won't fix these things either. There's nothing intrinsically wrong with trading information online with a group of like-minded people—foodies, cancer survivors, pro-football survivors. It makes the world that much more intimate. But if the majority of your social interaction occurs through a wire—if your life is so lacking in intimacy that you're looking to fill enormous life gaps online—your analog life needs attention, stat.

Don't pummel yourself, though, if you don't become a checkout-line chatter overnight. It's much easier to venture out in stages, starting with structured groups: a church, a softball team, a neighborhood committee. That way you'll have activities to fall back on when terror strikes. Volunteer organizations are perfect—an activity shared by a bunch of people in a charitable mood, just what you need. Or, get a part-time job tending bar; strangers will be paying to hang out with you.

If the mere thought of doing any of this gives you flop sweat, then maybe it's time to talk to a doctor about social anxieties.

Some more incentive to get out there: Socially, we are never judged as harshly as our fears tell us we are (junior high notwithstanding). Considering the amount of physical and emotional cellulite we all cart around, we *have* to forgive it in others. Check out the wedding announcements in your local paper if you don't believe me. Not exactly a New York model search.

Final incentive to keep your social life offline: Retreating into the electronic security blanket, like porn, can be the start of a downward shame spiral. You don't have the real thing so you settle for easy fakes, and you hate that, and you feel like a loser, and you erode your own confidence to the point where you don't have the nerve to look for the real thing anymore. How very sad.

"She has had a lot of painful experiences in her life, which to her means she has an unlimited license to complain to anyone who will listen."

6

SULKING

—

Good moods are good.

If it helps, I can t y p e   m o r e   s l o w l y.

Think about what puts you in a bad mood. Too much to do, too much traffic, not enough sleep, romantic disappointment, financial disappointment, job-loathing, the pissed-off feeling you get just thinking about all the things that piss you off.

What's the common element here? Powerlessness. You're at the mercy of time, at the mercy of other cars, at the mercy of the neighbors' roof work, at the mercy of the opposite sex, at the mercy of your creditors, at the mercy of the boss, at the mercy of being at the mercy of everything. We are all powerless to a certain extent, obviously, and most of us have our moods. Nevertheless, when things happen that we can't control, we can control our response. It's not much, but it's something. It's also why a persistent funk, particularly if it comes with whining, complaining or swinging at the moon, broadcasts to everyone around you that you've decided not to exercise that control—or worse, that you're using it to feel sorry for yourself. World 1, You 0.

Not that people need such a complicated reason to avoid you, when everyone knows that having a sulker around for one's entire life would be a total screaming drag. (If you're looking for compassion, try aisle 5.)

When someone you care about is down, of course you should reach out to help—and when you feel perpetually, intractably down, you should get some help for yourself. The sulking may be depression, which is common, treatable and real. There's no need to limp along feeling ashamed that you don't feel better.

Now that all the disclaimers are out of the way . . .

When you're assessing someone's merits as a potential partner, your primary duties are selfish—as they should be—which means no sulkers and no "you won't get *me* to a shrink" depressives. If you were hiring a driver, would you pick the one who knows where he's going and is making good time or the one who keeps hitting a tree?

There is an exception, though: If you're a man and you want to attract droves of needy, self-destructive women, sulk away. They'll think you're a poet. They'll think you're "brooding." They'll want to nurture you. They'll think if they only care for you properly, as opposed to all those awful family members and thoughtless teachers and abusive coaches and selfish ex-girlfriends who mistreated you ruthlessly (ruthlessly!), *then* you'll be the happiest man on earth. They'll make you the center of their universe. They'll never leave your side. They'll drive you nuts. You'll try to lose them and find the rest of us, but we will have long since fled in disgust.

"Why is it so difficult to meet a nice normal guy who's over five foot seven and has hair?"

7

LOSING PERSPECTIVE ON LOOKS

—

In *three easy steps*, you can do your small part to quell the hysteria over appearances:

1. Be rational about your looks. Make the best of what you've got using only subheroic measures, then don't look back.

2. Be rational about others' looks. Broaden the range of people whom you're willing to get to know. Every single one of us has watched friends get better-looking in our eyes as we grew to appreciate them

more, so it seems to be blatantly in our own self-interest to give less-than-bradpittlike prospects the same chance to ripen.

3. Stop trying so hard to be rational. If you try to be open-minded but the attraction just isn't there, then accept that without extensive personal remonstrations and move on. Looks *do* matter, after all; the point is simply not to generalize or to judge them too quickly.

Next. The less we gawk at this topic, the better.

"I plan on breaking up with him
if someone better comes along."

8

SCANNING THE ROOM FOR
BETTER PROSPECTS WHILE
WE'RE TRYING TO TALK TO YOU

—

If there's someplace you'd rather be, we'd like you to
go there.

"She takes one bite out of her main course
and says she can't eat any more."

9

PICKING AT YOUR SALAD

—

Statements you make when you order the *l'especial
lapin*, dressing on the side, nibble for two minutes
and declare yourself sooo full!!!!:

A. My appearance is more important to me than
enjoying life.

B. The more comfortable I feel around you, the more
I'm going to talk about my weight, worry about my
weight, ask you about my weight, try to lose weight,
get depressed about my weight. What I'm never, ever
going to do about my weight: make it interesting.

C. It's not just weight—my *entire life* is a monument to tired, girly stereotypes! (Especially lethal if you're a man.)

D. I'm aware of all the recent research that says dieting doesn't work, but I'm too dense to make the connection to my own life.

E. I have a chronic weight problem. One more bite and I will be huge.

The cool girl's guide to first-date food: Order a meat or fish slab. Eat it. (Unless slabs are the most expensive things on the menu. Then go for the ribs. Lick your fingers and I'll kill you myself.)

For one night, at least, a healthy attitude about food is better than healthy food.

"At what point
do you have to have
the 'status of our
relationship' talk?"

10

GETTING TOO
CAUGHT UP IN WHO'S
PAYING FOR WHAT

—

. . . Or what you wear, or on which date you're supposed to do this, or by when you're supposed to
know that, or whether you're allowed to talk about
your flesh-eating divorce. If you're absorbed by
getting all the strategic details right, you're getting
the whole thing wrong. And if you're turning every
detail of your relationship into The Conversation,

congratulations, you've found the most effective way to drain every fluid ounce of soul from your burgeoning romance.

This goes back to the dating-book issue. The details—your clothes, your conversation topics, your small but considerate gestures—are all a natural extension of you, your personality, your values, your beliefs (assuming you resist the urge to over-think or pick compulsively at each little thread of them). They are precisely what you need to show a person, for two reasons. You want your date to make an informed decision about you, and you want to make an informed decision about your date. How can this happen unless Real One meets Real Other? Artifice, "rules," strategies, analysis, do's and don'ts all mess with the natural chem-istry and that's the last thing you want, even if, especially if, that chemistry really blows. You want to know that upfront, now, today, THIS MINUTE—not when your various fronts give way to sick feelings two weeks after you started sleeping to-gether.

Okay, everyone, on three! A one and a two and—"Oh, I gotta be me ... "

Remember, if that "me" has problems, adjust the problems themselves, not the tie you picked out to conceal them.

"I am the type of person who
looks at bad things and thinks
something good will come
out of them."

11

STARTING SENTENCES WITH,
"I'M THE TYPE OF PERSON
WHO . . ."

—

". . . is really insecure." Even if you aren't, you're
going to sound that way when you manage to include
in one part of one sentence the fact that you define
yourself by your membership in a larger group, that
you've given the question of which group you belong
in a great deal of thought, and that you want whoever
you're with to recognize that you have this group
affiliation. Not good, not good, not good.

Say you're a woman who identifies more with men. If it feels as plain to you as breathing, men will respond to that. If you order dark beer just to say, "HEY LOOK AT ME I'M NOT ORDERING THAT GIRLY WHITE WINE," you're going to set off the trying-too-hard alarm in every guy in the room.

There are things you do well and do miserably. There are things you like and don't like. There are things you'd like to push out of a fast-moving vehicle even though of course you never would do such a thing. These abilities and opinions combine to make *you*—and they will speak for themselves, whether you let them or not. Let them. Don't feel the need to interpret the data for the person across the table, I'm this, I'm that, I'm whatever. If you're comfortable with your choices, you can sit back and let the other person decide what to make of them, even if that decision turns out to be, "Nah." That's because being comfortable with yourself means you don't need approval from everybody you meet. It's a good thing not to need, considering that a whole lot of people you meet aren't going to like you.

Let me guess—you're the type of person who can handle that.

"My good friend obsesses over this
guy. He never calls her, never asks her
for a date, plays games with her
(example: telling her to leave his
apartment at 3 A.M. after sleeping
with her)—however, she says he's
a funny guy and a good time
to hang out with."

12

THINKING WAY, WAY TOO MUCH OF YOURSELF

—

This would seem to be self-explanatory, but since
everybody who makes this mistake by definition has
no idea he's making this mistake (or any mistake at
all), I'd better explain it anyway. To a bunch of

people who are too full of themselves to realize that
I'm talking about them.

Onward.

To put a twist on the old, and strangely gross, saying:
We are whom we date. If you think way too much of
yourself, you're going to alienate the six billion or so
people on earth, give or take a few, with enough sense
to be repelled by your bloated sense of self. That will
leave you to choose among the few people you don't
alienate, the ones who buy your act—and therefore
have a bloated opinion of you.

The people who have this problem, of course, are still
waiting to see what the problem is.

Everything, that's what. If you want to know the
value of someone who has a realistic opinion of you,
spend five minutes with someone else who thinks
you can do no wrong. Everything you say to her is
brilliant! Everything you say is funny! She never says
anything brilliant and funny back! You might as well

date a throw pillow. Plus, anyone who worships you won't notice, much less call you on, any mistakes—and, guess what, you're making mistakes all over the place just like the rest of us. That means you're acting like a jerk and *nobody's tipping you off*. A raging egomaniac is a lonely egomaniac.

If, on the other hand, you've got an equal at the table with you when you're out with friends, then she'll have the presence of mind to kick you in the shin when you start that anecdote again about oh God I can't even bear to type it. It's a given that having quality classmates will improve our educations, talented opponents will improve our games and sharp coworkers will improve our productivity, so it shouldn't be a stretch to say that quality friends and lovers will improve our selves—both by playing to our stronger traits and by calling gentle attention to our ugly ones. The reverse is so clearly true: Poor companions feed our worst selves, fomenting anger and frustration and glassy-eyed boredom and leading to the non-choice between a life of quiet desperation or a life of restlessness, affairs and serial self-indulgence.

Is it me, or do I keep saying things that would make this life sound appealing to the exact people I want to talk out of it?

Perhaps the most persuasive argument for keeping high-quality company—and keeping the ego in check—is that someone who can stand up to you will be able to stand up *for* you as well. That's a strength you may one day need.

Yeah, sure, you don't need anyone's help with anything and that anecdote you like to tell at dinner parties is fascinating and if you get bored with someone, so what? Good for you—now go try to share this epiphany with your many devoted friends.

"My nineteen-year-old daughter
has a new boyfriend who is twenty-four
years old, has never held down
a consistent job, abuses alcohol, smokes,
hangs out at 'titty bars' and 'borrows' money
from her. I believe she is depressed about
her weight, with which she struggles, and
not [often] having a boyfriend."

13

HATING YOURSELF

—

Or, more of the dating-what-you-eat thing we were talking about in number 12.

Hating yourself is very bad. Going out expressly to find someone to love you is very worse, which is

why it amazes me that it's seen as the folk remedy for self-loathing. Even if hate is too strong a word, even if you're just not liking yourself much these days—or if you privately feel you're stupid or ugly or drinking too much or not funny in crowds or some other unlovable thing—you're going to attract everyone who agrees with your dim assessment of yourself.

Here's why. Since you're feeling unworthy already, being around good, strong, happy people is going to sound as appealing as a punch in the throat. (Step right up, everyone! Make me feel inadequate!) Of course, it's the good, strong, happy people who will invariably treat you the best, which is exactly what you need right now—but, given that low assessment of yourself, you're also reasonably convinced they want nothing to do with you, so you either avoid them or you put yourself down so endlessly and tediously when you're with them that they learn to do all the avoiding for you.

That leaves you looking for love among the only

people who don't scare you away: people who don't like themselves much either. Around them, you're a star, right? You feel much better now? Well, no. For one thing, you need their love and attention to keep you feeling special, and the minute you telegraph that neeeeed to other people—the minute you demonstrate that you won't leave, no matter what—you've invited them to find out just how much abuse you'll stick around and take.

No no, you think, your sweetie would never do that to you. Except you forget that he's got doubts of his own about his self-worth, which means putting you down can give him a tempting little boost. Meanwhile, with your doubts still raging, you'll be inclined to believe his putdowns, which will further weaken what little morale you've got.

The mistreatment doesn't have to be malicious either. Say there's a guy who's feeling less than stud-like, maybe struggling with work and unsure of himself socially. He finds a woman who is struggling with work and hasn't burned up the social circuit herself—and has a gentle nature that makes him feel like the street-smart and confident one. She'll stick around because she's a little too painfully aware of her own limits and secretly questions her ability to do better, even though she'd hoped for more than this Kmart Romeo. He'll hang on to her for dear life, too, to assure himself of a steady, adoring audience.

She will cling, he will cling.

She will translate her doubts about her attractiveness into jealousy and turn a deep emerald green if he so much as looks out the window at a passing car. He will reinforce these insecurities by dismissing her concerns, putting her down, treating her with contempt—all of which are subtle and sometimes unwitting reflections of his own disgust with himself. He's annoyed he's not with someone better; that's the easy explanation. But he's also afraid she'll leave him and fairly certain that, if she becomes more self-assured, she *will* leave him. What better way to keep her around than to send her the message that no one else would want her?

The definition of a good partnership is one that makes the members stronger than they would be apart, but in this case each of them has a vested interest in keeping the other weak. She will be unhappy, he will be unhappy, but both will be so weakened and spooked by the prospect of dying alone they'll be relieved they're unhappy together.

Of course, the mistreatment *is* malicious sometimes. Everyone knows domestic abuse is a widespread problem—so where do you think all those abusers get all those mates to abuse? From the deep well of people who are so busy feeling like dirt, so busy thinking, "I'm so happy he wants me!" that they tune out the voice that says maybe this is a guy they shouldn't want. Or a girl they shouldn't want. (Help, I'm being held by the thought police . . .)

It's a cruel and ironic thing that when we're at our lowest, when we're most vulnerable, when we're most deeply impressed by the opinions of others, when our sense of self and therefore our judgment is most compromised, *that's* when we go panhandling for attention. But that's our way, and all we can do is try to recognize it and tether ourselves until we feel better. Oh, and we can listen to our friends: They can be wrong about a lot of things, but the friends who say, "You let people treat you like dirt," are almost always right.

"When she gets trashed
she becomes pretty hostile, which she
never is when she's sober."

14

DRINKING TOO MUCH

—

The three most important things you can bring to a date are nice clothes, good judgment and interesting things to say. A few tee many martoonis and you'll be parting too soon with all three.

I'm referring here to the onetime, lapse-of-restraint kind of drinking too much, on the assumption that the habitual drinking-too-much issue is too obvious to justify the additional paper stock. Whether you're the one wearing the lampshade or your partner is, you're not dressed for anything good.

The occasional drinking-too-much issue may seem a little fuzzy, but there are some clear lines: If a person can't drink without going all the way to blotto or get blotto without getting hostile, there's a monster in there. Don't make excuses for it, deal with it—preferably at an AA or Al-Anon meeting.

"We ended up hooking up. We actually talked about it and decided there would be no strings attached. That's fine with me. What's not fine with me is the fact that now he doesn't talk to me anymore."

15

HAVING SEX BEFORE
YOU MEAN IT

—

There is, in fact, no way to make this point without sounding like a prig. So if I'm going to be the prig here, I'm going to be the prig with gusto: Stop having sex with people before you develop an exclusive emotional bond with them, you slut.

You may have your own sexual code, and you're entitled to it. Your sense of morality, of honor, of dignity, of taste—these are what you offend most when you wake up to a bad decision, so it's generally wise to resist outside influences and just do what your own senses tell you.

But it can't hurt to be acquainted with reality either. Regardless of what you believe, if you don't wait long to have sex, people in general still see that as cheap, and if you wait a long time to have it, people in general still see that as meaningful. So if you don't want to give the impression that you're cheap or that you're ready to commit to one person, don't have sex.

I know, you'll take that chance. But consider this, at least: If the guy you've been seeing introduces you to his friends, and if you discover to your horror that you click with one of those friends better than you ever did with the boyfriend, then which of the following two scenarios will intensify your horror: not yet having slept with your new boyfriend or having just slept with your new boyfriend?

Meanwhile, there are other realities about putting

sex before emotional intimacy that don't care spit about your personal sexual ethics—or anyone else's. Pregnancy is one. If a woman gets knocked up, the couple's choices are abortion, adoption, shotgun wedding or raising a child with only one resident parent, which I will agree is just as good as an intact family as soon as someone proves to me that a second parent is superfluous. Choosing one of these options, for a baby you created, is an enormous moral responsibility, yet when the sex partners— 'scuse me, "parents"—hardly know each other, what are the odds they'll know where the other falls on these fundamental issues? And when they find out, what are the odds they'll agree? Before anyone's pants come off, all women should assume they'll get pregnant and all men should assume the woman will want to keep the baby. Everyone can work backward from there.

Another ethics-proof reality is viral infection. Condoms slip and break, which puts HIV and hepatitis in play, and condoms also don't, ahem, cover everything. That makes two other sexually transmitted incurables—herpes and human papilloma virus (HPV)—available to anyone who has sex with an infected partner. Until there are vaccines to save us from viruses and ourselves (not necessarily in that order), we have to rely on trust. It's hardly perfect, but we hardly give it a chance to work either.

Here is what trust needs: Two moral people. Theoretically, two moral people could have a one-night stand before which they share reliable information about their health and their moral positions on abortion, adoption and childrearing.

Theoretically, a sweepstakes van could be a mile from my house on a mission to deliver to me a comically oversize check.

But if I said, "I think a sweepstakes van is coming" and I started spending massive sums in anticipation of my imagined winnings, you'd all think I was mad; I can't possibly know I've won until the van itself arrives, right? It's equal madness to rely on the morality of a sex partner—to risk your future, really—before you have any proof she is moral. That proof takes time. You need to see each other in action and watch for day-to-day signs of integrity. You need to see what value a person puts on the truth—to see, for example, whether he speaks up when he's been undercharged or whether he takes responsibility for his own mistakes. That value is the only guarantee you'll get that a lover is faithful to you or otherwise being honest. Think about it: Someone can *say* she's using birth control, but how will you know that's true unless you've witnessed in her a genuine respect for you, for other people, for the truth?

And the final reason not to sleep with someone without first developing an emotional bond is that a lot of us are a lot less ready than we think to hear the phone not ring.

"I meet a guy, maybe hang out with him, give him my number, he never calls—or he gives me his number, I leave a message and he never calls me back. Am I picking the wrong guys or do they all just lie?"

16

NOT CALLING

—

The number one whined-about non-gesture is the failure to call as promised—and it might be the only situation in which whining is fully justified. If you sketched out plans for next Saturday but you decide to go out of town instead, call to cancel. If you said you had a nice time, and you were lying, and he calls two days later and leaves a message on your machine to set up another date, and you want to ignore him till he goes away, don't. Call back, say no. If you're a guy and you just slept with a girl for the first time the night before, call her call her call her, just to say hello or just to say good-bye. If you end a date with, "I'll call you tomorrow," and as you heard it come out of your mouth you knew you wouldn't call her tomorrow, do what you said you would and call tomorrow. Just *make the damn call*. Even if you'd only be calling to say, "I'm sorry, I shouldn't have promised I'd call."

Bonus points for making the damn call: Once you've said "no" nicely, you're under no obligation to make or return a call to that person again. In fact, the decisive "no" is the kindest.

True, you get no romantic credit for blowing people off nicely, since the people who find out that you're a direct and thoughtful person are the ones you won't be seeing again because you just blew them off. Do it anyway. Think of the payoff as karmic.

"He began psychoanalyzing me
and psychoanalyzing himself, and
wondering why he could never get a date
and why all his girlfriends left him,
exclaiming that it was a miracle that I was
even on a date with him."

17

UNPACKING YOUR BAGGAGE
ON THE FIRST DATE

—

Things I think we can all stipulate about a first date:
You're with someone whom you don't know well but
find interesting enough to want to know better. Fair?

So if you're sitting across from someone new and at
least minimally intriguing and you can't come up

with one measly dinner's worth of conversation topics without cursing, lamenting or retreating into the comfort of some ex-something, you're wasting this new person's time. If you're *badmouthing* the ex, you're wasting yourself—both barrels.

Get the check and go home, and don't date again till you're over her. Or him. Or it.

There's no need to go overboard *not* mentioning things; two adults pretending never ever to have had feelings for anyone else in the past is a dangerous swerve into farce. Exes will come up naturally, so you might as well learn to set them back down naturally, too.

She: "I was born in Akron."

He: "An old girlfriend of mine was from Akron. Maybe it's my Mecca."

They: Change subject.

If you're asked about an ex, don't mistake that for an invitation to clean the emotional pipes. It's an invitation to be cool and gracious about your past and . . . very good, change the subject—even if that past had fifteen affairs before absconding with your best friend, your late mother's jewelry and the $500,000 she embezzled from your business to an island nation with lax extradition laws. It's also an invitation to wonder why anyone would be asking about your exes on a first date.

There is one exception to the don't-ask-don't-tell-much policy: If you've been married before, that should be out in the open before date one—unless there's some practical reason you couldn't exchange basic information, like you're on a blind date or you were at a bar with a bunch of friends and you asked your waitress out on a bet. (Hint: Tip well.) But even if the first date is your first chance to cover the basics, the fact of your former marriage is all you need. The ghosts stay home.

"She's quite pretty, but I am thoroughly
uninterested because she talks too much.
From the minute one meets her,
it's nonstop chatter."

18

FORGETTING TO
ASK QUESTIONS

—

Did you have a great time?

Did you marvel at how easy this date was to talk to?

Did you take twenty minutes longer than she did to
eat dinner?

Were you the only one ordering coffee?

Did you wake up hoarse?

Do you have any idea whether she has siblings, why she chose her career? Quick—cat person or dog?

Did she ever return your calls?

"I think that he needs to pay a little
more attention to me and at least try
to talk every once in a while."

19

CREATING AN
INTIMACY IMBALANCE

———

If he hears your deepest secrets before the entrees
slap the table, and you know none of his, why does
he need to be there? Wouldn't an inflatable date be
the same?

Actually, it wouldn't. An inflatable date wouldn't be
wondering why this person he doesn't know trusts
him with (or expects him to care about) her entire
life story.

People have a basic need to feel special and they look to their mates to satisfy it. Makes perfect sense. So if you're on an early date and you share your most private self with someone you barely know, that someone will make the following connection: He is a virtual stranger to you, and therefore your most private self is available to virtual strangers, and therefore you will have no intimacy or secrets left to make him feel like he's the special one whom you have chosen to trust. So he will bail.

Lay down your cards one at a time, slowly, alternating turns. Don't yell "FIFTY-TWO PICKUP!!!!" and expect him to care about the mess. He won't.

" 'Slurping' and 'shoveling' are the two words that best sum it up."

20

EATING LIKE A PIG

—

The upside of smacking your lips, chewing with your mouth open, licking your fingers, sucking liquid audibly from the glass, gulping, toothing your fork, clanging your spoon maniacally against the dish while you chase down every last edible molecule, picking your teeth, sucking your teeth and punctuating arguments with airborne food particles: Anyone who'll dine with you twice must really, really like you.

But you want to reward the faithful, not punish them. Ask a good friend to give you a barnyard-manners check. It's always better to let your ego take the hit, as opposed to the horrified face of the person you'd hoped to impress.

"So, I'm one week into a new relationship with a guy and for the first time ever, he seems to really dote on me, more than I do on him even. He's even mentioned coming home with me for Thanksgiving."

21

GETTING ALL EXCITED WHEN THE OTHER PERSON WANTS TO COMMIT QUICKLY, YESTERDAY, NOW

—

Having someone agree with you is always pleasant, and when the agreement is about how wonderful you are, it can be intoxicating—especially when you've felt alone in that opinion for quite some time. So, hey, enjoy it!

Just don't operate any heavy machinery. Anyone who sweeps in and decides you're the light of her life has to be treated with some skepticism (she said joylessly). At least at first. You've known you all your life, so you, naturally, have a nuanced opinion of what you have to offer. Therefore, you like to believe—we all do—that anyone who has a sudden, intense interest in you must somehow have picked up on all these nuances. But what can someone possibly know about you after a couple of weeks, a couple of months even? That you're nice to look at, nice to talk to and you don't give off a smell. Don't mistake promising for profound.

The risks when you do make that mistake run from simple to sinister. The simple one: that the excitement will die an abrupt and ugly death the moment you start learning substantial things about each other. A change of heart is common, even at normal speed—but it's a whole lot harder to take if you've lovingly pasted artifacts from all two of your dates together in your scrapbook (Our First Coat-Check Stub, 1/24/00 ☺).

The sinister one: People who quickly attach themselves to you often don't care to learn your nuances, ever. They want someone in the significant-other role to make them feel normal/special/powerful, and they have a preconceived notion of how you should play this role, and they'll resort to all manner of controlling behavior to keep that notion intact. (See number 44 on page 139.)

It's not as if you need to be on the lookout for emotionally imbalanced freaks every time your soul cries out for hearts and bunnies and butterflies. Just keep your foot in sanity's door. Resist seeing the new person sixteen out of the next seventeen days, or choosing the names of your children before you've hit the three-week mark, or giving him closet space before you've met even one of his friends. Romance is like alcohol: Pace yourself and you extend the buzz; get carried away and you wake up kissing tile on some mystery bathroom floor.

"I don't know if she has similar feelings about me, but I do want to find out. The catch is that I want to do so without putting the friendship at risk."

22

PINING SILENTLY FOR YOUR "FRIEND"

—

Having gotten this question now (click click click) SEVENTEEN MILLION times, I no longer answer it. But I did answer it for a while there, and saw the response go from long, to shorter, to shorter, to this:

If you are pining, you are not "friends."

Just tell the person your feelings have changed and deal with the consequences. In fact, if you're a man, confess *as soon as you feel them change*. Otherwise, the object of your affection will pick up on your unexpressed feelings (instantaneously—trust me on this) and will, consciously or not, read your silence as a sign of weakness. Not a great moment for your masculinity. Call it sexist, but I call it true: Women can get away with hesitation, men can't.

Say the "consequences" of confessing turn out to be your worst-case scenario: The feelings aren't mutual. You will feel a wave of awkward horror, but that wave of awkward horror will stay with you only if *you* let it. Take the rejection like an adult, be civil to the person who rejected you, laugh at being the butt of Fate's cruel joke, do the whole I-feel-like-a-doof routine. So you feel like a doof. How will you feel ten years from now if you never even tried? How sad that awkwardness is usually seen as the greater evil when it, at least, will pass.

"He shows up and says,
'So . . . whaddya wanna do today?'"

23

BEING INDECISIVE

—

"Uh . . . so . . . whaddya wanna do today?"

"Uh . . . I don't know . . . uh . . . what do you want to do?"

Stop! Stop it! Aaaagh!

Somehow, somewhere, word got out that people like to have their every whim catered to and so that must be the way to please a date: Do exactly what he wants. Well, maybe *he* likes to be introduced to something new once in a while. Maybe *he* gets tired of having to make all the decisions all the time. Maybe he finds it refreshing to know women who have minds of their own.

This much, I know: Indecision in men is a deal breaker. She draws from something primal that makes her wonder how a guy will ever drag home an entire buffalo carcass or defend the cave if he can't even pick a restaurant. A decisive man, on the other hand, is a magnet, for reasons that are hard to describe. Is it the sense that he has total confidence in himself? That he can be at the wheel in a snowstorm and you will feel safe enough to drift off to sleep? That the fundamental pieces of his life always have been there and always will be there and he still wants to make room for you?

Whatever the reason is, it's gone, pft, the minute a woman sees that she has to run the whole show. The strange thing about the prevalence of the do-what-ever-she-wants phenomenon is that men clearly get bored by a power vacuum, when they have to suggest everything and decide everything and do everything. So why don't they anticipate this in women?

Maybe it's all this new awareness of abuse that has men backing off and getting all squirrelly. Hello, "I'm in the mood for linguine" is not going to land you in jail (just don't break into her house and write it on her mirror with lipstick).

Still, the fear of appearing abusive doesn't explain waffling women, who are just as bloody annoying. Maybe people just don't want to sound pushy. But come on, it's not like it's either/or. One can express an opinion to someone else with an opinion without the use of force:

"I'll pick you up at eight then. Does Thai food sound good?"

"It does, but it gives me gas. How 'bout Chinese instead?"

"He's sleeping with two different girls and uses no protection with either of them, they're not faithful to him, and neither of them knows about the other."

24

HIDING THE OTHER TWENTY-SEVEN PEOPLE YOU DATE

—

You know what they say, do unto twenty-eight others as you would have twenty-eight others do unto you.

If you're dating casually, then there's nothing wrong with dating miscellaneously. In fact, if you think of it as life research, dating around is smart: You'll be much more confident in your judgment of people if you've drawn your opinions and experience from an array of sources. This is particularly relevant if you're fresh out of a convent/all-boys school/hyperconservative culture/multiyear dry spell, and the sum total of your research so far can fit on a Post-it.

Fortunately, if you do choose to survey all your options, it doesn't take much to do that guilt-free: Just keep it honest and keep your pants on. Not only is that the decent thing for the twenty-eight people you're seeing, that's also the right thing for your health and sanity.

If, on the other hand, you've got a conveyer belt next to your bed, you may:

A. Find it hard to trust people later on when you finally decide to get serious, since you know firsthand just how many people someone can be seeing/sleeping with on the side without arousing suspicion.

B. Find out one day that the person you've pretended to see exclusively is someone you really *want* to see exclusively and, lucky you, you get to keep up that initial lie happily ever after.

C. Adopt a virus.

"I love spending time with him
and he is absolutely terrific in bed,
but I don't really want a relationship
with him. He's into these
games and playing with my
head: doesn't call when he says
he will, cancels plans,
smokes pot like three
times a day."

25

BEING IN IT
FOR THE SEX

—

Frankly, I don't want to know what you're doing and
why. We're all adults here, more or less, and this adult
is a prude.

But at least make your actions consistent with what you ultimately want. If you set out on a physical adventure, expect the payoff to be . . . *physical*. Right! Very good.

There are a bunch of things you can expect from sex for the sake of sex—that the novelty will wear off, that eventually one of you will want more out of life, that you increase your risk of disease, that you will be having sex—but love? Respect? Meaning? I suppose it does happen sometimes. So do Powerball jackpots, but I'm guessing you still have a job.

"All of a sudden she disappeared—didn't
return my calls or e-mail or snail mail
—and said something about being
really sick, but now she tells me she had
lost touch because she was mad at me.
And here I was actually worried
about her health."

26

LYING

—

There are exactly the same number of reasons that
lying is stupid as there are reasons to lie. What a
cowinkydink.

Because you're ashamed of what you do for a living?
The person will find out eventually.

Because you have something to hide? The person will find out eventually.

Because you want to get laid now and you don't care who finds what out when? Disease, eventually, you pig.

Because you don't have the nerve to say "no" to his/her face? The person will get the "no" message eventually, after all seventeen calls go unreturned— and you will look like the coward you are.

Because you like messing with people? The people you mess with will have the last laugh, because they will learn the hard way never, ever to treat other human beings like dirt and will therefore not wind up dying bitter, despised and alone.

Because you never get caught? That's worse than getting busted. Every lie you get away with is a bit of lost faith in the truth.

If you're so afraid to confront the people you care

about that abusing their trust sounds more appealing—if lying seems like an appealing alternative to anything about your life—it's time to fix your life. For example, you're uncomfortable saying what your job is, so you pad your résumé when you meet people. That's your 800-pound clue to ask yourself if you *should* be uncomfortable with what you do. If your line of work is totally spiritually bankrupt, or if it's merely beneath your abilities, then listen to your shame and do something about it. Find a new job, learn a new skill, enroll yourself in night school. If the problem is that your job isn't suitably glamorous, then ask yourself if your priorities haven't gotten skewed. Doctor or dishwasher, an honest role in life well-performed is one of the most eloquent statements we can make about ourselves. Are you making that statement? Then stop apologizing for it. Anyone worth knowing will respect the pride you take in your work, and therefore respect you. That's the cliché version, at least. To get the true version you have to add, ". . . and the jerks will still underpay you, insult you and pretty much laugh in your face," but you can't squander your pride on them.

The same face-the-truth tactic applies if you're ashamed of your financial status, of mistakes you made in the past, of your physical condition: Change what you can, make peace with what you can't and let the masses think what they want.

"It has been three years since she dumped me. I still would like to talk to her, I think it is necessary for me to find closure."

27

HOLDING THE SINS OF THE LAST GUY AGAINST EVERY NEW GUY FOR THE REST OF YOUR NATURAL LIFE

—

You go to a restaurant. You find a bug in your salad. You:

A. Don't give it a second thought because it's a bug for God's sake. You're not going to die.

B. Complain, then celebrate. Free salad!

C. Complain, never eat there again.

D. Complain, never eat at a restaurant again.

E. Keep eating at that same restaurant and ordering that same salad and eating it one leaf at a time but only after each passes a rigorous five-point bug inspection. Talk about how uncomfortable you are with talking about your "lettuce issues." Cry. Leave a 10 percent tip.

F. Find a bug in your food at *every single restaurant you try* and fail to make the connection that you're the one with bugs.

How we deal with adversity might be the most valuable piece of information we can supply to potential mates. To any kind of companion, really. We form emotional bonds for stability because we're so much easier to knock over alone—and if there's one promise life holds, it's that it will take some mean shots at everybody. If you respond to even the pickiest little setback with a five-alarm blaze of hysteria, or if you carry around with you the scars of every disappointment in your past, you won't be much use to the team when the really big stuff goes down.

It's a legitimate question to ask yourself, if you feel like relationship poison but you don't know why: How cool are you when your battery's dead, your shipment gets lost, your boyfriend dumps you, your salad moves on its own? Are you good in a crisis or do you ratchet everything up to a panic? Are you some variation on a live-laugh-and-learner (A through C) or a high-maintenance breakdown already in progress? Will you make someone's life easier? Or harder?

"All he does is snap recently and I can't stand him. He says he is so tired from work and that he had a bad day and blah blah blah. I work, too, and I'm also getting my master's at night, planning a wedding and flying home every weekend to help take care of my grandmother who is dying of cancer! You want to learn how to let the little stuff roll off your back? Hang out in the cancer ward."

28

FORGETTING TO LAUGH AT YOURSELF

—

I think sometimes about those studies that say people live longer if they laugh on a regular basis.

My New Grocery List, courtesy of science:

Fruit
Olive oil
Fresh spinach
Salmon
Bran cereal
Skim milk
Beans
Beans
Beans
Beans

If you aren't laughing on a regular basis, I can't imagine you'd want to live longer, but I don't think that's what they meant.

Yet if you combine this fact about human health with the point in the preceding chapter about human life—that pain, loss and humiliation are our birthright—then you've got the formula for brilliant lifetime companionship: someone who can withstand all manner of misfortune and bounce it back as a punch line. Pain, loss and humiliation are also funny, when put in the proper perspective. What else would you want to do with it all, absorb it all till you snap? Deflect it onto others? Channel it all into golf? Sulk? People always say life is too short for something or other, but I say life is way too long to spend with someone who can't bring a little light into all that dark.

Finding someone who makes you laugh is ideal. Be your own goofball, though, and not only do you make yourself a whole lot more refreshing to be around, but you also take the pressure off yourself to be the vision of suave perfection at all times. Plus, laughs at your own expense earn you credit toward laughs at someone else's expense, which always help.

"We have a lot in common and get along
really well, except for this one area.
He likes to get his own way and is
very pushy about it."

29

WANTING TOO BADLY FOR
THINGS TO WORK

—

We get along great, except for that minor teensy-
weensyish okay PUNY issue about his treating my
needs like something he scraped off his shoe.

Why is it that when a relationship is writhing on the
ground with a massive sucking chest wound, so many
people preface their questions about it by insisting,
"We get along great otherwise . . ." I know men
who've done this, but my letters suggest it's still

mostly a chick thing—a chick thing *this* chick Does Not Get.

Bulletin: A failed relationship is not a failure. (Massive sucking generalizations about an entire sex, by the way, are a failure, in an intellectual sense, but I'm proud to say that I'm not afraid to fail.)

If the person you're with has a fundamental trait that makes you fundamentally unhappy, despite reasonable efforts on both your parts to work through the problem, then you *don't* get along really well and you *don't* have a great relationship. What you have, if you OPEN your EYES, is important insight on what you need to be happy—and what you currently aren't getting. So collect that insight, turn off the "I can mold him into the perfect man!" nurture switch and go.

"I have been dating my boyfriend since August 1998. I didn't find out he was married until six months later, after I called him and got a girl on his phone. She asked me who I was and I said a girlfriend; she said she was his wife and hung up on me. He is still married and I have a problem with him not getting a divorce. He says there are two reasons and he can't tell me. I do know that he does not have any children. He is illegal and I was thinking that he was trying to stay married to get his paperwork fixed."

30

DATING AFTER
THE LOBOTOMY

———

Please don't breed.

"I always thought that sports knowledge would work in my favor with guys, but many of the men I meet become hostile."

31

TRYING TOO HARD

—

Guy 1 was a birder so you bought binoculars and learned to distinguish one plover from another plover from a thousand feet.

Guy 2 was into NASCAR, so you got a Dale Earnhardt T-shirt, started referring to trailers as "manufactured housing," built a still and developed your own recipe for moonshine.

Guy 3 was a photographer with seasonal affective disorder, so you subscribed to *Photosensitivity Today*, read up on the latest advances in Vitamin D-fortified lighting and rewired his darkrooms at home and at his office.

Guy 4 was a Shakespearean actor, so you spent the next month at work reading the Bard's entire dramatic oeuvre covertly on the Internet while you alt-tabbed over to an online screenwriting course, wrote a screenplay for a half-period, half-present-day New York reinterpretation of *Henry IV, Part I,* persuaded Kenneth Branagh to sign on to direct it by showing up at his offices and doing a pitch-perfect Brooklynite Falstaff in a doublet of your own design, and then begged him to cast your Snookie in the lead.

Does this sound like you? Really? Or are you just saying it does because you think I'll like you if you agree with me?

Never mind.

People, we seek. Parasites, we eventually have removed (see number 4 on page 22). There isn't a lot more to it.

"I have these two friends who are in long-term relationships, and all they can talk about is what they want for Valentine's Day. They both want these particular pajamas, and they have to be a certain style, color, etc., and God help their boyfriends if they get it wrong."

32

BELIEVING IN ESP

———

Right, you know there's no ESP. You simply want the other person to love you enough to make an intensive multiyear study of every aspect of your character in order to develop the uncanny ability to buy you just the right gift.

And say all the right things when you're sad. And not ask you leading questions first thing in the morning. And know which calls to screen and which invitations to accept and when to say you look beautiful although your outfit has all the panache of a Salvation Army couch.

You think you want this hyperattentive mate—but when you get one, do you know what you do with him? Drop him and run screaming to the first man who ignores you. Ask anyone who considers himself to be faultlessly attentive to a lover's needs how many times he's been dumped.

If you want to spend your life with an independent thinker, expect a few off-the-mark gifts and misguided comments and the occasional weekend alone. If you want to spend your life with a footstool, find someone eager to invest the energy to account for your every whim.

"I'm dating a guy whose ex-girlfriend calls him frequently, and she called us and bothered us even while we were on vacation together. How can we stop her from continuing this harassing behavior?"

33

JUDGING PEOPLE IN A VACUUM

—

Some surprises need to cook for a while, but when they're ready, they pop out at you like a done piece of toast. This was one of those: We talk about romantic relationships as if they're an entirely separate category from other human interaction—and we don't even think it's weird.

It's weird.

I didn't get my mind all the way around this until I'd read a couple of years' worth of complaints about this guy's obnoxious family and that girl's harpy friends and this guy's clingy ex-girlfriends and hello hello hello, you don't see what this means to *you*?

His family's problems are his problems.

Her friends reflect her values.

He couldn't say "no" with a gun to his large Jell-O head.

These other relationships in a partner's life are actual-size blueprints for how this person behaves—and yet we routinely dismiss them as nuisances, exceptions, head-scratchers, whatever suits our needs at the moment.

We need to examine these relationships, closely. We

need to meet parents and siblings and see how they treat one another. We need to meet friends—new ones, sure, to see if there are any—but especially the old ones, to see if there are any. We gain all the more from seeing how someone treats a coworker, a boss or subordinate, though that's not always possible. How does she treat children? How does he treat your pets? Your stuff?

Here's a great one: How does she treat a waiter? What volumes that routine transaction can speak.

"We are so different from each other,
and argue when we don't do the things
that the other one likes to do."

34

UNDERESTIMATING
COMPATIBILITY

—

You are five. You are in the yard with your dollies.
Your new five-year-old neighbor walks up with her
dollies. Bam. Friends.

Friends, at least, until you're fifteen, and her criteria
for choosing dates turn out to be "is he male?" and
"does he have a car?" and you're developing a crush
on your (female) AP chem teacher.

What makes perfect sense when we're five (that enjoying the same things is a legitimate start to a friend-

ship) and act on when we're fifteen (that enjoying different things can end a friendship because our choices often reflect our values) seems to fall out of our heads when we're twenty-five. We act as if looking for someone to share our interests is too facile. Playmates? Humph. Soul mates! That's what we need.

But, but . . . if you don't share any interests, what are your souls going to do with each other? I mean after the first few months?

I'm not saying you have to spend every waking minute together (and, in fact, I'll be saying not to in a second). But if you're going to share a home with someone, you're already going to have to make the kind of effort that sharing a home requires, like keeping your mood swings in check and pulling your share of the household weight and remembering to leave the damn seat down. If it also requires effort to find things you can do together, or worse, if you're reduced to spending alternate weekends doing what the one wants and the other clearly doesn't, then the allegedly fun part of being together starts to sound like work, too.

Not a popular Valentine's Day card: "It's an effort just to be with you."

If you both have to work too hard to please each other for too long, then you each start to wonder privately where your payoff is and grow to resent the other's hobby as the reason you don't spend any time together.

A moldy stereotype by way of example: She's a gourmet foodie, he loves football.

She subscribes to *Je Mange* magazine, she puts away hours at the stove, she puts out five courses at a clip, she puts out a grease fire after she gets a little too caught up in the multiple-course action, she makes a giddy mess of every pot in the house even though she knows the dishwasher is broken and so the cleanup will have to be biblical. He starts with the local pregame at 11 A.M. and doesn't so much as twitch while the national pregame, the 1 P.M. game, the 4 P.M. game, the 8 P.M. game and then the highlights of the 1 P.M. and 4 P.M. and 8 P.M. games roll by.

She looks at him and sees another beautiful fall Sunday that he wasted indoors, and complains that football keeps them chained to the house every weekend for six months of the year. He thinks the kitchen was used to film a teenage splatter flick and complains that he'd have been just as happy with takeout Chinese—especially since she [expletive] knows the [expletive] dishwasher is broken. Both come to view the other's choice of diversion in terms of how it has injured them personally, then proceed to add up the hours of lost life and the degrees of disappointment to demonstrate the injury's extent. Both lay out these totals as moral arguments against each other's choices. At this point, it's no longer about hobbies or diversions, but about what each of them values in life. Both therefore guarantee there's no room for compromise.

He could, after all, invite his football buddies over to watch the game, and she could try out funky recipes on them, and he could clean up the kitchen when everyone leaves—but no, he's not going to clean up the mess made for something he never wanted in the first place.

They could go away for the weekend together and be home by 1 P.M.—or wait till his favorite team has a bye and go away then—but no, she's not going to rush back early from the countryside or in any way— horrors—schedule her life around pro sports.

Instead, she schedules a whitewater-rafting trip (nonrefundable deposit) for the day his team makes its first trip to the playoffs in franchise history. He agrees to go along just to make her stop yammering and then shows up three hours late.

(Their friends, meanwhile, can like them both tremendously and wonder why each can't just grant the other his happiness and be done with it. And wonder why they both go to such lengths to deny that their situation is unfortunate, or even unusual.)

The saddest part of torture-by-incompatibility is that it's so unnecessary. There isn't only one Love of Our Lives—and whoever said there was should be slapped. There is the love that'll go antiquing with us, the love that won't but will amuse itself while we go, and there's the one that makes us feel like bubblebrains for wasting an afternoon rummaging through other people's castoffs.

When the love we've found is of the latter variety, shouldn't we put it back and keep looking? Of course, a movie-watching, tofu-eating, dog-loving football fan with a dark sense of humor might seem like a rather tall order when you'd be content at this point with a guy who didn't insist on picking his teeth with a straw right there at the table after every goddamn meal. But what isn't too much to ask is for you and your partner to have enough common interests to make weekend planning a low-stress enterprise—and to have enough respect for the not-common interests to defer to them without moping.

One type of compatibility to avoid, please: crutch compatibility. When you both play seamlessly into each other's weaknesses, grab your boots and run for the hills.

"I have tried bookstores, and never fail to
get the sense that I am the only one looking
for anything other than books."

35

CHOOSING YOUR ACTIVITIES
BASED ON CAREFULLY
CALCULATED ODDS THAT
YOU'LL FIND LUUUV

———

See number 34 and tell me how you're going to find
someone with compatible interests if you keep
doing stuff you don't particularly like to do, but
think you should be doing to meet women (see also
number 31).

What do you *want* to do?

Meet women. Ha ha.

If there were no women, what would you want to do?

Die. Okay . . . whack off. Then die.

Naturally. Say you already have a woman. What would you want to do then?

Hang out with her.

You're pathetic.

Your point?

If you had a girlfriend already, and if she were away on business for a few weeks, and if you had no intention of cheating on her with another woman while she was away, and assuming you didn't care to spend your time sitting home gazing at a blank wall, *then* how would you choose to spend your time?

Oh. I get what you're doing.

Thank you.

Think of the things you enjoy doing purely for you. Now do the things you enjoy doing purely for you. The following is likely to occur: You will meet other people who enjoy doing the same things you do.

The following might well occur: One of them will be a hottie.

The following will occur, a rises-in-the-morning, bet-the-dog-on-it certainty: You will be doing something you enjoy.

Women or no women, isn't that better than gazing at a blank wall, waiting for someone to cruise-direct your life?

"He has moved straight into a casual relationship—we hang out at his house to watch movies or TV."

36

EXPECTING SOMEONE TO CRUISE-DIRECT YOUR LIFE

—

Finding and loving and settling down with someone feels like an exhilarating accomplishment, and while we all have our own ways of celebrating, there are a few common ones: getting fat, dropping that whole "kindness" act and behaving as if you're excused from having a social life till death do you part.

Treat marriage as the culmination of the whole friend-gathering process and what do you get? The two of you. Every. Day. Either that or you'll have one of you shouldering all the responsibility for getting out there for the two of you, meeting new people for the two of you, setting up dinners for the two of you, planning vacations for the two of you, wondering why there even need to be two of you. You might annoy your partner more if you gain a hundred pounds, but lying around waiting to be amused is weight of a different sort. Deadweight.

People bitch ceaselessly if they're the sole source of affection or housework or cash, but given the sheer volume of people tapping their feet and checking their watches while they wait for "the one," not enough credit is given to how obnoxious it is to peg your entire schedule on whatever "one" shows up.

There are already so many excellent reasons to develop roots outside of your romantic life that I feel like I'm shortchanging them by suggesting you develop them merely as a way to help find somebody. But your friendships, your interests, your connections are, absolutely, what make you an attractive catch in the first place, and to let them languish on the "mission accomplished" theory is no different from chucking the treadmill and refusing to wash your hair the minute you utter your vows—it's a classic bait and switch. No fair.

"Should I just recognize what a superb man he is and give up on the fairy tale?"

37

GETTING SO CARRIED AWAY WITH HOW WELL YOU GET ALONG THAT YOU FORGET ABOUT THE SEX

—

Actually, I have no proof that forgetting about sex has ever happened. But people do often write that they're tired of looking or they've been burned by passionate relationships, and they've got this great person now who's "incredibly kind, sweet, talented, down to earth, educated, hard-working" and in love with them, and would it be so wrong to marry this person for whom they feel not the tiniest spark?

And I wonder why they're asking me when I'm not the one who has to sleep with the guy. All I can do is shudder involuntarily and offer a friendly reminder of the worst-case scenario: You marry your lukewarm love . . . and then you meet someone who's incredibly kind, sweet, talented, down to earth, educated, hard-working and, oh no, hot. Since life is dark and cruel, that someone will be the best man. What do you have then? New dishes, a wrenching moral dilemma and a honeymoon to make your skin crawl.

There is no guarantee, of course, that you'll meet this other person—and a lust-free but happy union wouldn't require a new entry in the annals of marriage. But if you hold out for someone you love completely, steamies and all, and if you eventually get married, and if that steam just dissipates with time as steam will do, then you'll have much better perspective on the occasional and inevitable crush that comes along. You'll know from experience that the new crush, too, would dissipate with time—and then you'll be able to weigh the transience of the crush against the permanence of your marriage, along with all the no-doubt-wonderful things it entails. That's what makes a crush not tempting.

You, in the same crush situation but in a marriage sans steam, will have this: A big fat "what if?"

"I asked my boyfriend to give up
an important trip with his friends
and family, and said if he went then we
were over. He got very emotional,
apologized and said he was still going.
I'm feeling guilty for being so demanding,
but I don't want to ignore this if it
is a signal that he doesn't care
about my feelings."

38

THINKING IT'S ALWAYS
ABOUT YOU YOU YOU

—

The funny thing about Me Me Me Land is that it's
not the domain of the arrogant. Excuse me—not
solely the domain of the arrogant. It is also peopled

by those who have been kicked around some and who have decided they won't be kicked around anymore. Resolving to stand up for yourself is admirable—but subtlety can sure take a beating in the process. Admitting fault? That's out. Compromising? Out. Letting the little insults slide? Out. Giving in? Oh my, out.

No one holds her ground like a recent ex-doormat—for the same reasons, oddly enough, that an arrogant person does: Each little surrender to someone else's needs or wishes becomes a little surrender of self and is therefore unacceptable.

Of course, anyone who has seen marriage up close recognizes that a refusal to surrender, ever, is the marital passport to hell. If you haven't found the middle ground between protecting your own interests and grinding your heel into someone else's, then you should do the cosmos a favor and just stay single.

Granted, when it comes to reconciling our own needs with someone else's, a healthy balance can seem like a narrow target. We concede one thing to a partner and we credit our emotional generosity and our unshakable sense of self; we concede one thing too many and we credit the fact that we're whipped. It's the head-scratcher behind so many couple crises. In a long-distance relationship, is it the strong one who uproots and moves to the other's city, or the weak? Are you the hero if you set your career aside to raise the kids while your spouse climbs the rungs, or are you a pushover? Are you the rock if you ignore a spouse's mood swings, or are you the resident boot scrape?

I can't answer that for you, you can't for me, and we can't know the answers ourselves till we get there. But we can all get our minds around . . . soup. Truly—it's a pretty good metaphor: You are one ingredient, your partner is another. Each of you can be identified as part of the mix because neither overwhelms the other, but it's the blending of both that makes the recipe great. Idn't that thweet?

"I have a friend who has been messing with
a married man since she was twenty-three.
She's now thirty and is still waiting
on him to get a divorce."

39

BELIEVING FOR A SECOND THE PERSON YOU'RE CHEATING WITH IS GOING TO DUMP THE SPOUSE AND MARRY YOU AND LIVE HAPPILY EVER AFTER AND NEVER CHEAT AGAIN

—

Please.

"My girlfriend wants to spend every
single minute together. I've had the
'I need more space' talk, but she only gets
angry with me and says I'm being selfish."

40

BELIEVING IF YOU DON'T
SPEND EVERY WAKING MINUTE
WITH SOMEONE, THEN
CLEARLY THAT SOMEONE
DOESN'T REALLY LOVE YOU

—

I got claustrophobic just typing that.

Scenario: Couple reaches the nine- to twelve-month
mark, the urgency-cooling stage, the prime breeding
ground for massive insecurity. She senses the cooling,

they both do, but instead of her using the scientifically proven two-plus-two method to conclude they're at a natural stage in any relationship, she chooses to question his devotion to her.

Great idea.

Part of the cooling is his gradual reconnection to his friends, whom he neglected a bit when he was in the throes of hormonal surge but now feels rational enough to enjoy seeing again. So he sees them again. Occasionally—NO GOD NO DON'T SAY IT— without her.

The question she formulates to address this egregious turn of events: "Shouldn't he want to be with me instead?" The question I formulate to address this egregious it's-all-about-me-istic question: Shouldn't you want to see your friends, too? Were all those people you knew B.S. (Before Snookums) just keeping the seat warm till you found Him? I suggest you go ask them what they think of this.

The argument for getting out there and maintaining old ties is the same as in number 36: These friends, these interests, this life you built B.S., are what made you the person he found attractive. Now that you've found him, great, spend time with him—but not so much time that your life outside of him withers and dies. The things you do independently both grow out of and feed into your personality, and if you decide you don't need that independent life anymore, you're essentially choosing to be nothing more than somebody's other half. I don't know about you, but my left half pretty much takes my right for granted (unless there's an itch it can't reach)—and neither half can tell me anything I don't already know.

As if that weren't self-defeating enough, abandoning old friends is also shallow, thoughtless and disloyal, not to mention insecure, because why else would you be doing it except to keep full-time claws on the mate? The next step, asking a mate to abandon friends on your behalf, is not only insecure but also self-centered to the extreme. Not two of the more impressive statements you can make to a person you'd like to impress.

"He's jealous of the time
I spend with them and questions me
whenever I see them (which isn't often).
When I confront him because I feel
restricted, he tells me that it's only
because he loves me so much."

41

GETTING JEALOUS

—

Jealousy is the single most obnoxious act in Lovedom—and second place? See that speck on the horizon? That speck is using a telescope to try to locate second place.

Jealousy means:

A. You don't trust the person you're with to

i) prefer you—unless you are the only man/woman on earth.

ii) behave.

B. You view everyone else as competition in the Who's the Most Attractive Contest—and you don't trust yourself to win unless you get to guide your sweetie's hand when it's his turn to vote.

C. You are completely irrational.

D. Either that, or you believe whiny accusations are the best way to make your partner happy. (Under the circumstances, I'd go with D. At least you can pretend that you've got good intentions.)

E. The only control you have over the relationship is the hands-on, no-you-can't-go-to-that-party-without-me control.

F. You feel you need control (see B), and are therefore an extremely high risk to be an abusive partner, physically or emotionally or both. People who do what I do are supposed to advise anyone with a jealous partner explicitly to dump that partner NOW.

G. You are such a pain in the ass.

A little flicker of jealousy can indicate there's something going on you should know about, but that only works if you are never otherwise jealous. How much faith do you put in a burglar alarm that goes off when the wind blows? Even if you do trust the alarm, you check the doors and windows—once—and go back to what you were doing. You don't wait at the door with a gun.

If you were raised to believe jealousy is a sign that you care about somebody or vice versa, get over it (and sue whoever raised you). Not only will jealousy say all the aforementioned ugly things about you, but if you don't put a leash on it, it will also have the bonus effect of forcing your partner to answer constantly to your various charges—charges that, as you know, can't be proven unless they're true. (Please describe for me what definitive photographic proof of a person not cheating would look like.) So a perfectly innocent partner will be incapable of proving innocence, which means you won't ever really believe the defense, which means you will keep accusing, and the innocent partner will get really, really tired of this and dump you, which means you will have achieved exactly the thing you most feared.

If you were cheated on and you're jealous because you haven't found a way to trust the person again? Leave. It's over.

A love partnership is a simple transaction: You send love and you receive it. If you don't believe someone could love you—if you're so insecure, so uncertain of your worth that you think someone will drop you the minute you allow him to meet other people—then you may be giving love, but you aren't accepting the delivery. That means you aren't a true partner. If you're plagued by doubts about your worth, then you have to address them; there is nothing anyone else can say or do that will get rid of them for you. Just ask all the anyone-elses you've been torturing all these years with your utterly groundless suspicion.

"When I asked her not to read
my personal writings without speaking
to me first, she got mad and said that
she has a right as my girlfriend
to read them. She said there
should be no secrets."

42

SAYING
"WE HAVE NO SECRETS"
WITH A STRAIGHT FACE

—

So you told him about that erotic dream you had about Sam the Butcher? Sure you did. Just like he told you all about the crush his best friend had on you until this guy decided you smelled funny and that was a surprisingly effective turnoff.

Question: Why do you need to know everything? You have a right to know what his day-to-day life is like now, plus a greatest-hits version of his past. Not only the various children or ex-spouses or felonies he may have floating around out there, but also whether his childhood was happy, what he wrestled with as he got older, how he chooses his friends. The rest of it, the dreams and dark thoughts and near misses—that's all just part of his wiring, and as long as the lights come on okay, it's not your place to mess with it.

There are such excellent reasons not to. Say, for the sake of argument, that you do believe you have all of someone's secrets researched and labeled and tucked away in your mind. Congratulations! You're DELUSIONAL—and, I'd bet, deathly afraid that you'll be blindsided by some truth you don't know, that some skeleton will pop from a guy's closet just as you're starting to trust him.

The strange thing is, by assuring yourself that you know all of somebody's secrets, you have a false confidence that puts you at a much greater risk of being leveled by something you missed. A mistress is an obvious example. If you're certain your Bubby would never ever cheat on you, then you're going to miss all the preliminaries—the faraway look in his eye, the giving up too easily in arguments, the brightening around new people in a way you haven't seen in years, the hanging around later and later at work—until the truth just falls on your head.

You might as well just put on your jammies, curl up with the fact that no one person can completely know another and be open to whatever surprises ensue. You can do your basic research on a person, but at a certain point, love, friendship, any kind of human interaction becomes a matter of faith. Call it informed faith, but it's still faith. You're not making the leap alone though—anyone you deal with leaps right along with you—so no one really risks more than anyone else. Sometimes the risk pays off, but when it doesn't, it can't always come as a shock and it can't be the end of the world.

"Breaking up did
the trick: We now get
along great."

43

FEELING THREATENED BY
THE FRIENDLY EX

—

This has been an unending source of entertainment
for me since I started writing my column:

In one corner, we have Hate the Ex letters, in which
the Current Girlfriend feels deeply threatened by
Ex-Girlfriend, who has remained on the scene as a
friend. Popular topic.

In the other corner, we have the Spark Is Dead letter,
in which half of a long-term couple complains of

losing all sexual interest in the other half. VERY popular topic.

Hello, and welcome to Connect the Dots! If the people we date have such enduring sexual power over us that we can't be trusted to speak to an ex much less befriend one, then why is it that so many of the longtime couples I hear from are frantically trying to relocate this power, this fizz, this feeling that they're more than just . . . friends?

Newness, mystery, suspense—these are what excite us, and the more familiar we are with someone, the less excited we're going to feel. That's why when sparks die, you can't just break out the paddles and jolt them back to life, even if you love someone immensely. What are you going to do, will yourself to forget things about the person until you feel all crackly again? Coming soon, couples' amnesia therapy! One swift blow to the head and you'd marry her all over again.

True, it's not unheard of for exes to get back together for an old-time's-sake one- (or two- or three-) nighter. But that tends to come close on the heels of a breakup and is more part of the breaking-up process than the ignition of something new. If you're micromanaging your boyfriend's relationship with his ex-girlfriend six years after the fact, you're probably wasting your time. Besides, simply trusting him seems much less exhausting.

The exception would be if you've never been introduced to his mystery ex, or if she doesn't make an effort to like you, or if the "friendship" is the unstable resolution of a grisly (and therefore still-passionate) breakup. In that case, be conscious of his loyalties. Note that I did not say, "Be a jealous, possessive, cornered little shrew." Simply take note of whose feelings he accounts for first; if they aren't yours, bail.

But if a new boyfriend and his friendly ex-girlfriend conduct their friendship out in the open, and especially if the ex-girlfriend is eager to meet and befriend you, those are your cues to be extremely laid back about their relationship—even to encourage it. If you need another reason to be mellow about the ex, consider this: You score major mensch points if you act like it's fine by you. Extra credit if it really is.

"When I got upset, he black-mailed
me by saying he would tell my parents some
personal details about our relationship that
I didn't want them to know. He says that
he did it for my own good."

44

MISSING (OR IGNORING)
RED FLAGS EVEN THOUGH
THEY KEEP THWACKING
YOU IN THE FACE

—

From childhood we're told—at least we are now—that
each human being is a unique and precious flower,
that there's no way we can be fully understood or
appreciated if we're generalized, stereotyped or otherwise thoughtlessly lumped.

It's a lovely idea, but it fails to account for the fact that, at some level, we're just a predictable bunch of lab rats. Thank God for that; our behavioral consistency is what allowed the people who work with abusers and their victims to recognize that controlling, insensitive jerks come in roughly one form. The description follows below. It was compiled from information provided by various domestic violence organizations,* but is by no means limited to men (statistically, the majority of batterers) nor to predicting violence alone. The items on this list could just as easily describe the woman you're seeing right now who, if left un-dumped, is destined to make you the kind of miserable only fifty years of unflinching marital dominance can make.

Emotional withholding: Not expressing feelings; not giving support or compliments; ignoring you; not

---

*From "Domestic Violence: The Facts," used with permission from Peace at Home, Boston, www.peaceathome.org; supplemented by information copyright 2000, David L. Gilles-Thomas, Counseling Center—Student Affairs, SUNY Buffalo Counseling Center, University at Buffalo, The State University of New York, http://ub-counseling.buffalo.edu.

respecting feelings, rights or opinions; sulking or getting angry when you initiate an action or idea; becoming angry in response to any sexual and emotional frustrations.

Verbal abuse: Name-calling, mocking, accusing, blaming, yelling, swearing, making humiliating remarks or gestures.

Intimidation: Invading your personal space—sitting too close, speaking as if he knows you much better than he does, touching you when you say not to; rushing you to make decisions through guilt-tripping and other forms of intimidation; threatening to withhold money/attention; forcing you to adapt to sudden swings from cruelty to kindness.

Possessiveness and isolation: Preventing or making it difficult for you to see friends or relatives; monitoring phone calls; telling you where you can and cannot go and how you should dress.

Abuse of authority: Always claiming to be right (insisting statements are "the truth" or "reality" or "logic"); telling you what to do; making big decisions for you.

Disrespect: Interrupting; changing topics; not listening or responding; twisting your words; putting you down in front of other people; saying bad things about your friends and family; seeing himself as smarter or socially superior.

Abuse of trust: Lying or misleading; withholding information; cheating on you; being overly jealous.

Broken promises: Not following through on agreements; not taking a fair share of responsibility; refusing to help with child care or housework.

Minimizing, denying, blaming: Making light of behavior and not taking your concerns about it seriously; shifting responsibility for anything bad to other people, to you in particular.

Economic control: Interfering with your work or not letting you work; refusing to give you money or taking yours; refusing to let you share any of the expenses of a date and getting angry when you offer to pay.

Self-destructive behavior: Abusing drugs or alcohol; threatening suicide or other forms of self-harm; deliberately saying or doing things that will have negative consequences (e.g., telling off the boss).

Harassment: Making uninvited visits or calls; following you; checking up on you; embarrassing you in public; refusing to leave when asked.

Violence: Hitting you; destroying property; threatening to hurt you or others; mistreating pets; forcing sex; using or threatening with weapons.

A partner need not have all these traits to be considered controlling; having several of them is reason enough to worry. And once you recognize them, don't rationalize them away by saying things are okay between you "most of the time." If someone were like this to you all the time from the first day on, how long would you stick around? The key to controlling behavior is the kindness in between, the promise of how great things could be if the other stuff "got better"—which, of course, it can't, because the good and the bad are all part of the same effort to control you. When it comes from an emotionally manipulative person, "I can't imagine life without you" isn't a beautiful romantic statement; it's the setup for "If you leave me I'll kill myself." You can't just pick and choose what you want to believe. The flowery moments and the tense moments are both calculated to keep you around and keep you submissive.

Better than any checklist, though, is your gut. Does it say something's wrong? Guess what. Something's wrong.

"He said that if he wanted
to talk to someone, that's what
his friends were for."

45

PLAYING IT SAFE—MEN

—

Pop quiz: Are your girlfriends ever as bright as your friends?

I suppose if you like your women fluffy and uncomplicated, that's your business. But you should know, dinners with the two of you are *torture*.

Yes, this *is* about me.

So here's more from me—or I should say from us, the ones you're torturing at dinner with your arm-candy girlfriends. We don't get why someone so bright, so engaged by a good political fracas, would want to spend the bulk of his time with a member of that (until now) mysterious 40 percent of Americans who can't name their own vice president and the 60 percent who think Rommel's a kind of cheese.

When we don't know why you're seeing somebody, do you know what that means? That means we're left to make up our own reasons and, as you know, we're not very nice. We're thinking that your masculinity can't handle a woman who stands at intellectual eye level (no, it's not only women who think this). We also think it's pretty ironic that you date beneath you so as to conceal your fragile manhood and yet dating beneath you is what exposes your manhood as fragile.

But then we think, maybe the fragile-manhood theory sounds a bit pat. Picking out one, narrowly defined insecurity is like finding a mouse in the basement. What are the chances there's only the one? If a man dates bimbos because a relationship between equals involves too much emotional risk, he probably also runs scared from real emotional bonds with men, too. The latter is simply easier to conceal: He can surround himself with tough, intelligent men—and share with them his deepest, most personal insights about sports.

Tip: Next time, think twice before you leave to go to the rest room.

"She fishes for friends in local bars
and nightclubs, and ends up in
dead-end relationships with
high school dropouts."

46

PLAYING IT SAFE—WOMEN

—

Pop quiz: Are the people you hang out with—friends and boyfriends—ever as bright as you?

Women don't do the topical friendship, not with the skill or frequency that men do. That's why, when they're avoiding intimacy out of a fear of getting hurt, they tend to date *and* befriend people who are beneath them. Intellectually, at least; you can argue that in most relationships, "safe" or otherwise, we seek out our equals emotionally.

The only time we really notice this, though, is when someone functions on a high level professionally, say, or physically or academically, but struggles emotionally—and therefore makes romance or friendship choices that make society at large say, "Huh?" What the bemused observer sees is a lawyer dating an underemployed short-order cook. What's really there are two people who are both a bit shaky on this whole intimacy/future thing and who choose just to duck the whole issue together. Sad.

"She is a wonderful, well-adjusted
person and is an incredibly loving presence
in my life. Problem is, my girlfriend
and I are not of the same religion,
and my parents are dead-set
against the relationship."

47

LISTENING TO YOUR
FAMILY AND FRIENDS
AND IGNORING YOUR
FAMILY AND FRIENDS

—

This is where knowing who the hell you are comes in
handy. If you've got a solid set of your own values to
work from, you won't get caught in the classic how-
could-you-date-this-person guilt-wringer.

Of the myriad ways families and friends will find to meddle in the mating process, faith makes the best example because it's taken as such common and legitimate grounds for meddling—and for the Romeo/Juliet in question to feel irreconcilably torn. But is it? If he sees faith as a make-or-break issue, then he lets the girlfriend go—in fact, he never lets things get this far in the first place. If his parents see faith as a make-or-break issue, then he has to decide if his parents' values are a make-or-break issue. But he's already indicated they aren't by getting serious with this girl in the first place. Granted, some people will date outside the faith or culture on the assumption that they can keep things light, and suddenly find themselves in love. But even then, to those who know their own minds, the choice will be clear either way.

The problem this guy has, the reason he's torn, isn't faith at all. It's that he's not comfortable enough with himself to support his own choice. That, in turn, makes him vulnerable to the opinions of every strong figure in his life, regardless of whether that figure has his best interests at heart or rides around on a broomstick.

Families and friends are a priceless source of information, but only after you've set the value of what they have to offer. Are you Mommy's bestest boy? Don't ask her to judge who's "good enough" for you. Has your sister resented every breath you've drawn on this earth? Listen to her advice and then go do the opposite. Is your friend on her fifth marriage? Take the legal advice, skip the romantic. Trusting your own judgment is how you know when to trust others'.

On one subject, though, friends and families almost universally excel. They do so well, in fact, that we should all vow never to tune their opinion out: They can tell if you're happy. You think you can tell for yourself—but then you give your capacity for denial too little credit. So if one of them sits you down and says, "You don't seem like yourself when you're with your boyfriend," listen. If one of them sits you down and says, "I've noticed you've been tense lately," listen. If one of them sits you down and says, "I'm worried about you," listen. If five of your closest companions have to sit you down and block your exit from the booth to tell you they fear for your safety, *listen*—and then change your locks. Then give each of those great friends of yours a big, wet kiss.

It is the source of endless frustration, for this spectator, at least, that so many people ignore their friends and families on these fundamental truths—and yet they choose to listen when they bring home fiancés who don't have as many advanced degrees as they do and are told by the resident snobs that the glaring intellectual deficit will surely doom the marriage.

Some observations are insightful, some are verbal flatulence. Helps to know the difference.

"My mother-in-law redoes
the chores after I perform them,
up to and including actually dumping
out a pot of water and refilling it after
I had filled it for pasta. Right in
front of me. As if I am too stupid to
have done it correctly."

48

TOLERATING AN ADULT
WHO WON'T STAND UP
TO HIS PARENTS

—

Mrs. Murphy's law: Whatever she can do to annoy
her child's mate, she will.

Mrs. Murphy's corollary: If that child won't stand up

to Mommy early, he won't stand up to Mommy ever and you will go out of your mind.

Clearly, there are wise, supportive parents who defy the in-law stereotype and support their kids' judgment on mates—if only because they have fresh memories of being tortured by *their* in-laws. My mother-in-law was so embittered by her husband's mother that she promised me that if her son and I ever fought, she would automatically take my side.

Such is the power possessed by a mate's immediate family. In fact, my mail suggests that most evil-in-law stereotypes barely dip a toe in the river of horror that the real stories create. Not that this came as a shock; a parent's proudest accomplishment is usually his child, so when you ask that parent to entrust his little work of art, his two- or three-decade labor of love, to an often youthful third party, you can't expect tension *not* to ensue.

But you can, if you're sick like me, be perversely entertained when it does, particularly between wives and their mothers-in-law. Few men seem to grasp the territorialism that comes wired in the human female and that manifests itself in a visceral protectiveness of the rites of Home. A woman who has created her nest is not going to look kindly upon the presence of a female who barges in and tinkers with that nest. We like our cabinets this way, we like to prepare our food that way, and have our philosophies about where the wet towels should go—and this includes women who are about as enthusiastic about living in captivity as great white sharks. When an unauthorized female decides it's her place to challenge the judgment behind these ways . . . oh do the fangs come out. Our own mothers can cause this reaction, too, if they're the ones choosing to push all the buttons. But it's the *other* mother, the husband's mother, the knower of all things best for her little boy, who's the barbarian at the gate.

It may be the most intense, but mother-on-daughter-in-law violence obviously isn't the only kind of in-law friction. All combinations of parents side against all combinations of children-in-law and vice versa. Regardless of who's antagonizing whom and why, it's emotionally corrosive—and utterly preventable. When a man and a woman commit to each other, to share their lives or home or name (whichever comes first), the two of them alone have a vote in their lives together. Each of them is also responsible for enforcing that limit with his or her own family. If a father criticizes his daughter-in-law's child-rearing philosophy, then the son needs to explain that they're his children, too, and that he and his wife have made these choices together. If a woman's mother clucks at the way her son-in-law spends money, then the daughter has to explain that these decisions aren't the mother's to make.

The solution is easy to type, but, for some people, extremely difficult to execute. A son conditioned to answer to Mommy will be loath to say no to her and will therefore stand inertly by while his mother, if she so chooses, peck-peck-pecks away at his lovely and outraged wife. Know this early: A true adult answers to himself. Marry an adult child who still answers to his parents and your whole marriage will answer to them.

"She's very insecure,
but I think when we're married
things will be different."

49

EXPECTING MARRIAGE
TO FIX A PROBLEM

—

See above, and witness the greatest premarital
howler of all time—unless he intended "different" to
mean he would soon get to wake up with that insecurity (moodiness/instability/[obnoxious trait here])
every day for the rest of his sorry life.

Jealousy and insecurity are the easiest problems to
rationalize away like this, because the victim can tell
himself that the marriage will ease any doubts she
has about her preeminence in his life. Great think-

ing! Because no husband's ever been accused of having an affair! Or been interrogated under the hot lights of the front hallway after coming home five minutes late! Or had to sever all his platonic friendships with women! Or been forced into adopting the mantra, "I was *not* flirting with the babysitter... I was *not* flirting with the babysitter... I was *not* flirting with the babysitter... I was *not* flirting with the babysitter"!

But jealousy's just one example. The same is true of any gaping behavioral wound your partner might have: marriage will make it *your* gaping wound. Feeling neglected? Wait till you're both ten years older with a mortgage, dog and children. Feel like you're being suffocated? Wait till you're both ten years older with a mortgage, dog and children. Hate that you're dating a mama's boy? Wait till you're married to one and you're never good enough for him in his mother's eyes, and you're never important enough in his, and your needs get dropped like a bag of dirt until the day she dies, WHICH SHE NEVER WILL, purely out of spite.

The moral of the story: If you're considering marriage, don't look deep into her pretty green eyes and ask if you can imagine life without them. Look deep into your problems with her and ask, "Am I ready to make these permanent?"

"Deep down, I like that he'll learn
that I'm not taking his shit
and get it together."

50

THINKING YOU CAN
OR SHOULD
CHANGE SOMEBODY

—

And about those problems between the two of you: If you look deeply into them and say, "I can *fix* them!" you belong in a special category of arrogant. Or is it stupid. I get them mixed up sometimes.

I'm not so idealistically bankrupt as to think problems can't be fixed. They can, but only if you've got some clue as to who should be fixing what.

Say the two of you have a problem with the way you've been getting along. No matter what it is, part of that problem is your responsibility and part is hers. Even if it seems one-sided, such as, "She's a narcissistic freak," it's still a half-and-half deal: She's the narcissistic freak, and you're the genius who chose, out of all the women in all the world, to date a narcissistic freak.

So you sort out which part of the problem is your responsibility and which part is hers. Then you put tape down the middle and you *stay on your side*. For example: You do not say to yourself, "I can make her not be a narcissist." (See what I mean about arrogant vs. stupid? It really is hard to tell which one that idea would be.) What you do say to yourself is, "I will not tolerate her self-absorption [your part], and if Barbra responds by showing more sensitivity [her part], then I won't have to dump her [your part]."

Same goes for all you women who believe you alone hold the nurturing power to make brilliant husbands of substance-abusing, job-hopping, bed-hopping, poetry-spewing, sloppy excuses for men. Every time he does something bad and you yell and scream (or whimper and whine) but *continue to date him*, you reward the bad behavior. Reward it, and you effectively encourage it. Encourage it enough, and you guarantee it. The only one "changed" here is you—you've adapted to pleasing a jerk.

"I'm tired of doing all the
damn housework and having
to beg for his assistance. The
thought of spending the rest of my
life with him is more depressing
than the thought of spending
the rest of my life with
my cats."

51

USING "MATE" AND "MAID" INTERCHANGEABLY

—

When you leave your coat over a chair and your dishes in the sink and your shoes wherever you took them off and the empty shopping bags on the counter and the empty toilet paper roll on the holder and the old newspapers on the coffee table, who do you think puts them where they belong? Elves? Elvis? Don't call it an "inability to see dirt." It's disrespect.

"I've been dating a guy for about five years,
and I'm getting antsy because
I want him to marry me.
Should I give him an ultimatum?"

5²

THROWING AROUND
MARRIAGE ULTIMATUMS

—

What you want: True love, happily ever after.

What your ultimatum will get: No love at all, or a match made at gunpoint.

Congratulations!

When you want something, do you just stand there demanding that someone give it to you? Or do you go get it? You have a relationship that you believe is at the marrying point. If you're happy with the life you've got and you want to make that happiness official, propose. If you're not happy, if your life feels stagnant and you think marriage is what it needs, it isn't (see number 49 on page 158). Also, ultimatums are passive; you're putting the responsibility for your unhappiness into someone else's hands. This is *your* unhappiness; *you* confront the source.

"To get back at him,
I started messing with
his brother."

53

ACTING ON YOUR
REVENGE FANTASIES

—

... will always, without fail, *guaranteed*, tell the world you're a loser. You are the one who cared more about the relationship. You are the one who didn't have anything in life to fall back on. You are the one who lacked the dignity and strength to take rejection in stride. You are the one we call "pathetic."

A true revenge story: A woman "gets back" at the man who dumped her by ... sleeping with all his friends!

Not only do all these friends now treasure her as they would a used Kleenex, the ex-boyfriend is questioning his sanity for getting involved with this unstable freak slut in the first place. (He should have doubts about the integrity of his friends, too, but it rarely works that way.)

Way to go, babe.

Next time, don't get even—get better. That'll really kill him.

"I generally turn them down, as it is really unappealing to me to date someone who has already been through half my girlfriends."

54

OVER-FISHING THE POND

—

Even if your motives aren't the most pathetic ever (see number 53 on page 168), passing yourself from one friend/acquaintance/coworker to another to another isn't the pathway to bliss.

I am constitutionally opposed to attaching rules or numbers to romance. Number of unreturned calls before you give up, number of weeks before you can sleep together, number of minutes you can stay on the phone with a guy before you sound too eager—

these are the Ho-Hos of the information world. Trace nutritive value, at best.

But there is a number I like: two. As in, the number of people you can credibly date within one social/professional circle. Say you're drawn to one person early but, as time passes, you're slowly drawn to another. That, you can get away with. Happens all the time.

But if more time passes and you're drawn to a third, then good luck persuading Love Object Number 3 that she's special when she's already seen you, up close, tell Love Object Numbers 1 and 2 they were special, too. Everybody knows that sleeping around cheapens sex; likewise, relationshipping around cheapens intimacy. And, in a way, that's worse: A disposable body sounds almost benign up against a disposable soul.

"Part of me just views him as pathetic,
sitting in his den with one hand on
the computer mouse and the other
hand . . . well, I won't go there."

55

STOCKPILING PORN

—

Three years, thousands of letters and not one documented case either of a woman with a sizable porn stash or of a guy *horrified*! to find porn sites on his wife's computer. Not one rumored case. Not one fake case.

Maybe you're keeping her to yourself.

So, boys, here is what women are saying when they run across that box you just can't part with (all from real letters): "Sick." "Pathetic." "Cheap." "Disgusting and annoying." "A sexual mess." "Freaked me out." "Degrading." "Animalistic." "I am sickened and disgusted."

Ooh, *baby.*

"Guys I know who get porn mags are less sophisticated in bed . . ."

. . . less sophisticated in bed . . . less sophisticated in bed . . .

I hear an echo . . . echo . . . echo . . .

"Can the marriage be saved? Good question. Do I want it saved? Good question."

I'll need a shower after I type this, but I will concede that the occasional randy magazine for the occasional randy male is hardly worth the trip to my soapbox—especially if the photos are arty and the articles fig-leafy and no one ends up in a meat grinder. Maybe you could throw it away when you're done?

Still, it's hard to describe the revulsion many women feel (and, to their credit, a lot of men) when they see a facsimile of a female, comically rendered in silicone, being used as a sperm receptacle. But it's easy to describe the effect of that revulsion in women: an abiding distaste for *being* that receptacle. You like plastic dollies, you get plastic dollies. Porn as self-fulfilling prophecy.

Obviously, some women (anecdotally, a small minority) don't mind porn, and some are even into it. *With you.* Not in lieu of you, and not with your entire mail-order past in some closet. So, can you throw that box away? Good question.

"My husband cites examples of
how unloved he feels and how he is
No. 2 (behind my thirteen-year-old son)
instead of No. 1 in my life. I do as much as
I possibly can every day to show him
I love him. He is not No. 2, even
my own son knows that."

56

BEING A SINGLE PARENT AND HAVING SCREWED-UP PRIORITIES

—

When you create a child and choose to raise him, you sign on to protect him and stand up for his interests until he's old enough to look out for himself. Non-negotiable and not open to interpretation. This translates into simple priorities: kid(s) first, you second, remainder third. If you mess with this order—specifically, if you put the child anywhere but first—then anyone with good parental instincts will be quickly and deeply repelled. So you'll be left with to-hell-with-your-kid guy, as described above.

Don't fear being alone. Fear him. Fear the weakness in you that makes you so deeply crave the presence of someone in your life that you'll let anyone into your life, regardless of how toxic. Or better yet, get some counseling and fix the weakness. And in the meantime, please stop breeding.

"He and his fiancée talked many times
about calling off the wedding since
they were having so many problems with
their relationship, but the plans have been
set for about a year and her parents have
already put a lot of money into the wedding
(including giving them a very generous
engagement gift, which has been
used to buy a new car)."

57

BUYING A PAINTING BECAUSE
IT MATCHES YOUR SOFA

———

It's a *metaphor*. I made it myself.

If you look far into your future and see yourself as

married one day, you're pretty much like the rest of us. If you look five feet into your future and you see yourself as married and you don't even have a candidate, you're pretty much a judgment emergency. You're taking a mass-produced thing (sofa/marriage) and building (your room/life expectations) around that—and flip-flip-flipping through the lovingly created, one-of-a-kind things (paintings/lifetime companions) until you come across the first one that fits your existing criteria (matches the sofa/agrees to marry you).

So what do you have left when the couch gets old? A big ol' painting you bought to match the . . . oh.

"He is afraid of leaving his fiancée
for me because he thinks I won't stay with
him and then he would be alone."

58

RULING OUT THE POSSIBILITY
THAT YOU MIGHT ALWAYS
BE SINGLE

—

I have it on good reader authority that "Don't worry, you'll find 'the one' when you least expect it" is the most condescending sentence in the English language. So when someone complains about perpetual singlehood, I try to be sensitive to that: "Well, at least you already have china and crystal."

I'm not going to pretend we aren't, on some level, programmed to seek sexual companionship. But if you've ever had a bad version of it (cringe! cringe!), you've seen the beauty of being alone. Then again, if you've ever had a *good* version of it, you've seen the beauty of being alone. Marriage has rewards I won't torture you by listing here—I am, for the record, a huge fan of the institution—and still, anyone who shares a life with someone is lying if she says there's nothing about single life she misses (or she's choosing to forget what she misses about it). And, of course, you can't ignore the number of people who enter marriage with the same high hopes as the rest of us, then hit the exits like naked people from a house on fire.

So, please, a little less idealization of being married— and, to go along with that, a lot less stigmatization of being single. Having been both, I'd rate the quality of these common life configurations as follows:

1. Happily coupled

2. Happily single

3. Unhappily single

1,074. Unhappily coupled

I hear endless complaints that our society is inhospitable—even outright hostile—to people not in pairs, but my response to that is, so? Change society. Explain to your married friends how thoughtless they're being when they organize only "couples" things. Challenge corporate or government policies that discriminate against singles. Make a daily, persuasive statement with your own life that you're not just a half-empty glass. There are almost as many single adults as there are married; you might as well throw some of that numerical weight around.

Still, the best response to being single—the only response, really—is, "So be it." Or one of its variations, "Hey, what can you do?" and the always comely, "Shit happens." What *can* you do? Bitch, whine, wait for your life to start—or enjoy what you have while you have it?

To nudge that attitude along, here are some things single people should never take for granted: making your own decisions—great stuff, I could stop the list there. But then I'd leave out the surface perks— viewing habits, eating habits, reading-in-bed habits, decorating-in-floor-to-ceiling-purple-chintz habits; and the profound ones—where you live and what house you live in and how you live within it. Eight hours of undisturbed sleep, bliss bliss bliss. If there's a mess, it's *your* mess. Ice cream for dinner! Cool. No sectioning off holidays to appease the needy in-laws! Cooler. No compromising on the future you see for yourself. Coolest.

Consider what happens when you find no joy in being single or when you're dissatisfied with your life in general: You can never know for sure if you really like a person or if he's just filling a vacancy. It's only when you've made some sort of peace with yourself that your judgment becomes reliable. Then you can look at your already happy life and decide, does this person add enough to justify the compromises?

Once again, I balk at reducing a healthy lifestyle to just another way to get dates, but, once again, I'm going to do it anyway. If you're out there enjoying the life you were dealt, other people will enjoy you. They will want to be with you. They will buy you large gems. They will want to keep you to themselves. They will not be able to entirely because you love your life and you're not going to give the whole thing up for anybody. You will keep the gems though.

"I've tried sport and social clubs,
coed softball leagues, cooking classes,
dance lessons, new hobbies and blind dates.
I've had my single experience and I'm
at a point where I'd like to meet
my mate and start building
some memories."

59

LOOKING FOR LOVE

—

Don't worry, you'll find "the one" when you least expect it.

Emphasis on the least-expecting and not the finding, which, for all either of us knows, might truly never occur.

Expecting is for tangible things. You expect babies to be born and ovens to work and guests to show up at eight, but looking for or expecting love reduces it to another appliance you can acquire. When have you ever gone out specifically to look for a mate, seen someone who fit the specs you envisioned, gotten acquainted, had your feelings reciprocated and eventually gotten married?

I guess I just find it difficult to believe we can take such an enormous, dynamic thing, get a rough idea what it looks like, put on our coats and go fetch it. First mistake is that you have *no idea* what it looks like, you can't until you see it, and so if you're looking for something else, who's to say you won't miss the real thing entirely?

Second, as you know if you've ever turned your house over trying to find something, looking can become an all-consuming passion—and when you don't find it right away, it becomes a madness. Before you know it a search for your car keys becomes a house-wide ransacking. If three hours of playing Find the Keys feels like a noxious waste of time, imagine three years of playing Find the Wife.

Meanwhile, this "thing" you're looking for is not a "thing" at all but a feeling, only a small part of which you actually control. You choose your clothes and your attitude and the paths you'll travel—but you have little say in the paths you cross. So why even try? Why not travel your path for your reasons? You'll have a general sense of where it will lead, which means you'll have the satisfaction of moving your life in a direction of your choosing—and you'll have that satisfaction regardless of what else you pick up (or not) along the way. If you happen to run into love and friendship, all the better. And the thing is, you probably will: I can't underscore this point enough, that the sight of someone who has both a clear direction and an open mind is a thoroughly appealing one. Maybe because we all want a little of that attitude ourselves.

One caveat: The clear direction without the open mind is a thoroughly *un*appealing sight. We should always be wary of people who are in single-minded pursuit of something—anything, really. The career ambitious, the socially ambitious, the Olympic ambitious—the only seat they offer the other people in their lives is the backseat. The goal comes first. If you're the single-minded one, keep in mind the lesson learned by countless famous people, in public, time and time again, about the perils of wanting one thing at the expense of all else. They win, they celebrate, they make the Wheaties box, they have nothing else now to guide them or give them purpose, they are last photographed arriving for their third drunk-driving arraignment. We are not built to bear the weight of a single defining purpose—few of us are, at least. Something about us craves more.

I harp on this because career ambition and athletic ambition are no different from marital ambition, from wanting marriage sooo badly that the person you choose is secondary. Not only that, but you set yourself up to feel crushing disappointment every morning you wake up single—and feel crushing disappointment when you finally "win" and wake up married, only to realize no marriage could possibly support the weight of all of those great expectations.

Same goes for people who put their social lives on hold for careers because they're young and they think they can, or because they've given up on their disappointing private lives. They're forming a new kind of divorce statistic: They burn out, or "multitask" themselves into a Xanax bottle, or chuck it all and buy a B-and-B in Vermont, or get so lonely and awkward, they think all they can do is work. Expect too much of any one thing and we do seem to lose our balance.

So that's it? All these issues, one boring answer? Balance balance balance. Like the world needs another book on that. Can I call it "bawance"—a full and varied life, lived with a sense of humor—and pass it off as new?

Whatever it is, the first step toward getting it is to shake off any narrow or limiting goals, like "marriage and family" and "gold medal." Next is a step back to view all the bits of your life, so you can gather them up into one all-purpose, far-reaching goal. A good trick is to think of what you'd like as your epitaph and guide your life toward that. I've got one I like so much, I want to buy it a beer: "I took the life I got and I lived the hell out of it." Then I take the third step: I laugh at myself, because my idea of living the hell out of life includes putting on sweatpants, watching a movie and screening my calls.

Please don't say I'm arguing against marriage and kids or gold medals or butt-kicking careers. I say go, get them, why not? I'm arguing against a vision that's *limited to* them. I'm arguing against the idea that there's only one way to be—paired off—and there's only one way to get there—to transform yourself into what everyone else says is ideal. An ideal should be strictly personal. It should be you, in all your unique glory, minus the angry/selfish/self-destructive/insecure/petty behavior that drives the rest of us nuts (see numbers 1 through 59). When we aren't hobbled by our own hang-ups, we have few true limits: our creativity, our moral obligations to one another, our range of ability, our capacity to function before we need another paycheck (and in my case another nine or ten hours of sleep) and the whims of law enforcement. Frankly, to limit ourselves any further is poor life imagination.

Speaking of a rich and imaginative and varied life: I've got one waiting, you see. And if you'll excuse me, I'm going to go live the hell out of it. As soon as I find the remote.

ABOUT THE AUTHOR

Carolyn Hax is a columnist for the *Washington Post* and author of "Tell Me About It," a syndicated advice column for readers under 30. She is a Harvard graduate and a 10-year newspaper veteran, and lives outside Washington, D.C., with her husband, Nick Galifianakis, who illustrates her column, and their dog, Zuzu.